AFTER
THE
BLOOD
BATH

AFTER THE BLOOD BATH

*Is Healing Possible
in the Wake of
Rampage Shootings?*

James D. Diamond

Michigan State University Press | East Lansing

♾ The paper used in this publication meets the minimum requirements of
ANSI/NISO Z39.48-1992 (R 1997) (Permanence of Paper).

Michigan State University Press
East Lansing, Michigan 48823-5245

Printed and bound in the United States of America.

29 28 27 26 25 24 23 22 21 20   1 2 3 4 5 6 7 8 9 10

LIBRARY OF CONGRESS CATALOGING-IN-PUBLICATION DATA
Names: Diamond, James D., author.
Title: After the bloodbath : is healing possible in the wake of rampage shootings? / James D. Diamond.
Description: Michigan State University Press : East Lansing, [2019]
| Includes bibliographical references and index.
Identifiers: LCCN 2018050629| ISBN 9781611863314 (pbk. : alk. paper) | ISBN 9781609176105 (pdf)
| ISBN 9781628953732 (epub) | ISBN 9781628963748 (kindle)
Subjects: LCSH: Mass shootings—United States. | Indians of North America—Violence against.
| Indian reservations—United States.
Classification: LCC HM866 .D53 2019 | DDC 303.60973—dc23
LC record available at https://lccn.loc.gov/2018050629

Book design by Charlie Sharp, Sharp Des!gns, East Lansing, Michigan
Cover design by David Drummond, Salamander Design, www.salamanderhill.com

 green
 press
 INITIATIVE

Michigan State University Press is a member of the Green Press Initiative and is committed to developing
and encouraging ecologically responsible publishing practices. For more information about the Green
Press Initiative and the use of recycled paper in book publishing, please visit www.greenpressinitiative.org.

Visit Michigan State University Press at *www.msupress.org*

In memory of
the innocent victims
of mass shootings
wherever they have fallen.

CONTENTS

FOREWORD

Robbie and Alissa Parker

The ripple effect that commences immediately following a mass shooting reaches far and wide. At its epicenter lies those most directly impacted: the victims and their families as well as the families of the perpetrator(s), moving outward from the same point of origin in disparate directions. Left in the void is a pain that never fully heals. Questions that will never be answered. This void and these questions leave us to wonder how to move forward. We know this because we are one of those families. Our daughter, Emilie, was killed at Sandy Hook Elementary School in Newtown, Connecticut, on December 14, 2012. She was only six years old.

As the ripples continue to careen outward, they affect communities, states, and eventually the entire country. Hardened hearts are softened. An overwhelming sense of sadness motivates many to perform countless acts of kindness toward surviving victims and among one another. Money is raised, celebrities perform, and for a moment it seems as if something occurred that can bring us all together and finally unite us. Then the ripples continue.

Too often after such tragedies we hear that there is not a playbook on what to do after such an event. By now we know that is not true. The playbook consists of expressing shock that such a tragedy could even take place. Victims are identified and remembered. Tweets are released in droves with thoughts and prayers. Politicians are eager to jump back on top of worn-out soap boxes only to yell toward a group of their supporters, all while turning their backs toward other groups, which are screaming in opposite directions. Citizens rush to one side of the field to stake claim as to where they stand among those that totally agree with them. Judgment and blame are ordained quickly and unapologetically at those left to assume responsibility. Almost as quickly news stations launch hour after hour of circling talk and debate that, in the end, leaves one feeling a sense of vertigo more than with answers or understanding. All this is done seemingly according to a schedule, with each returning cast member appearing on cue. Yet when the smoke clears, we look around and realize that no significant change has taken place. With the number of these tragedies increasing, it is time for a new playbook to be written.

In this book, James D. Diamond uniquely assesses the topic of rampage murders from educational, professional, and personal experiences. In doing so he has managed to bring a different and, quite honestly, a fresh perspective to the roles played after a mass murder has taken place. This is not a book intended solely to point out flaws and mistakes of others, but to offer possible solutions and areas that need further evaluation.

Naturally, after crimes of such atrocity, our tendency is to find who is responsible and demand justice. Unfortunately, in many cases the person(s) responsible are gone, leaving no one to directly accept blame or enact justice upon. The focus is then redirected toward those that were closest to the perpetrator, who in turn are looked at with suspicion and culpability. This leads those with potentially valuable information to become withdrawn, silent, and defensive.

What many people fail to realize is that victims and their families need more than blame or justice to satisfy what is causing their hearts so much pain. We quickly learned after the shooting at Sandy Hook that what we were really looking for were answers: answers to how this happened, what could be done to prevent it from happening again, and most importantly, how we could heal. Through our experiences we have found that when we focused our energy on healing, the answers we were looking for came naturally.

Our quest for answers about how this shooting happened eventually led us to speak directly with the father of the young man that murdered our daughter. After the shooter took his own life as well as his mother's, who was his caretaker, the shooter's father was the closest surviving relative to whom we could ask our questions. We are grateful that he was willing to meet with us and provide what information he could. By meeting with him we learned that he too was searching for answers, felt sorrow for what had happened, and was prepared to do what he could to help bring any meaningful information to light. Had he felt like he was being attacked or demonized in any way, he could have robbed us of valuable information that we needed in our healing process as well as in the formal investigation.

The benefits from answers obtained in such settings have the potential to reach far beyond suffering family members. That knowledge can help mental health professionals, law enforcement, schools, and communities better understand what happens before a rampage murder occurs, and therefore, provide clues to inhibit one from happening in the future. Understanding warning signs and triggers, and how to identify them, might allow us to help potential perpetrators long before a tragic event takes place.

In rare cases where perpetrators are apprehended, the drama of assessing accountability and justice plays out in a lengthy criminal justice process. Court rooms are a place for cold hard facts, expert opinions, and where a game is played between lawyers that involves trying to either enact or minimize punishment. The emotional toll a drawn-out court case takes on a victim's family can be excruciating. Many times, a family is unable to start their healing process until after a case is finalized. Court rooms are not a place for healing for families or communities after a mass murder has taken place.

We feel indebted to the work James put into this book. His ability to weave his experiences as an attorney, his work with indigenous cultures, and his personal relationships with victims' families has allowed him to shed light on a topic that is starving for new solutions. The ideas expressed in this book can potentially start a process where accountability and justice are served, and truth and answers are found. Hopefully the ideas expressed here will lead, above all else, to an understanding that healing can be attained by anyone whose life was forever changed by the ripple effects following a heinous crime

PREFACE

y journey on this road began with a series of personal observations as an experienced criminal lawyer, of the postscript of recent rampage killings. My close personal and professional ties to Fairfield County, Connecticut, and academic ties to Tucson, Arizona, where two recent rampage killings occurred made these observations natural: it was hard to look away.[1] My personal observations of rampage killings led to research of whether instances had occurred among indigenous communities. When one was discovered, the research revealed a distinct difference in how offenders and family members were treated.

The distinction of the response to the rampage shooting on the Red Lake Reservation of the Red Lake Band of Chippewa Indians pointed me toward a study researching the historical traditions of criminal dispute resolution among indigenous peoples around the world. The methodology utilized a triangulated qualitative research methodology (original observations and investigations, third-party source materials, and pattern recognition) incorporating periodicals, textbooks, and legal case analysis, digesting those from a journalistic, anthropological/sociological, and legal mindset, then creating a paradigm consistent with social science investigations. My findings are organized around case studies with analysis that incorporates both traditional legal case reporting and the practices, mores, and traditions of indigenous peoples.

The parents of a six-year-old first grader murdered at Sandy Hook Elementary School, Alissa and Robbie Parker, graciously agreed to participate in this book, giving me their perspective and then writing the foreword. I discussed the Sandy Hook case with the chief prosecuting attorney who investigated it, although he was not asked for input. I have been part of large audiences listening to the victims (or family members) of the Tucson incident, and I have corresponded with surviving parents in other cases. In one instance I relied wholly on personal observation and trial transcripts: when I was an expert witness in a murder trial.[2]

This book examines the typical American reaction to the tragedy of rampage killings. It also examines the interplay between offenders and their families and victims and their families. It discusses an emerging and unreported trend, the desire for some level of reconciliation and healing between the families of rampage offenders and the families of their victims. It reports a distinct difference in how some American Indian communities treat rampage killers and their families. My research finds a weakness in academic attention to date in the community and judicial responses to horrific crimes.

This book then looks to the roots of American Indian approaches cited in indigenous historical evidence. I describe an institutional weakness in the Anglo-European judicial model in how it responds to the aftermath of heinous crimes. I explore the adaptation of certain practices from indigenous peoples as a method of contributing to healing, closure, and reconciliation following heinous criminal behavior. I further explore the possibility of incorporating face-to-face, interpersonal interaction between mass-shooting victims and their families and offenders and their families. In this regard, this book makes a unique contribution to the field of study.

Chapter 1 is an introduction. Chapter 2 defines the crisis of mass shootings or rampage murders, as it is referred to and explained here. Three mass shootings are examined in grave detail: Columbine, Virginia Tech, and Newtown. A complete listing of the names of the victims of these three tragedies is included in appendix 1. In chapter 3, mass shootings on American Indian Reservations, particularly at Red Lake High School, are examined in detail. Patterns in the aftermath of mass shootings and responses by the community, by victims, and by their families are examined in chapter 4. The chapter includes reports of courtroom testimony of mass killing victims or their family members. An examination of the history of indigenous dispute resolution among a select group of peoples is detailed in chapter 5. The recent trend of family members of rampage killers meeting with family members of the victims is discussed in chapter 6, as is the subject of forgiveness, the foundation of forgiveness in religious belief, and the application of forgiveness to rampage killing. Navajo peacemaking, along with other modern approaches to restorative justice and therapeutic justice, is described in in chapter 7.

Chapter 8 includes my recommendations for a way forward. As one part of that, I ask a couple of important questions: What changes are necessary to prepare lawyers and judges to accomplish the reconciliation, healing, and the talking-things-out approach suggested here? To what extent are the subjects of mental health or mental illness taught to law students?[3] The spotlight on mass shootings certainly has put these subjects on the radar screen for educators. As law schools adapt to a changing world and changing profession, the observations discussed in this study, as well as the subjects of therapeutic and restorative justice, are all worthy of greater future consideration and attention.

■　■　■

My research led me down a number of other paths that did not find a home in this study, or that were mentioned but not treated with detailed analysis. Three are worth mentioning. After discovering that the Red Lake Band of Chippewa Indians paid money to the family of the offender, Jeffrey Weise, I researched victim compensation and governmental legal definitions of what constitutes a victim due for compensation purposes. A good beginning to the discussion on the topic of compensation is Kenneth Feinberg's *Who Gets What.*[4] When rampage killers die, should their families be eligible for institutional compensation for bereavement counseling and funerals? I scratch the surface on this important subject and include it in my recommendations, but the subject is ripe for further academic study.

The second topic not included is the criminal prosecution of parents whose children commit atrocities, namely the enforcement of parental responsibility laws. I touch on the subject but, like victim compensation, it too is a subject for another day.

The third subject not discussed in this book is the substantial disparity of mass media coverage given to mass shootings occurring at schools like Columbine High School and Sandy Hook Elementary School versus occurring on or near American Indian reservations, like at Red Lake and Marysville, for example. There are a number of explanations for the disparity, one being the desire and ability of the

Red Lake Tribe to close off the reservation to the press. A critical race analysis of the coverage, however, is worthy of academic attention.

A note about terminology: I use the terms "American Indian" and "indigenous peoples" when referring generally to the indigenous peoples of North America, and occasionally "Indian." Most indigenous peoples prefer to be referred to by the name of their specific tribe (e.g., Cherokee, or Tohono O'odham), and I do that wherever possible. While others prefer the term "Native American," a clear preference does not exist, nor should it be expected to exist; they are both oversimplifications with colonial connotations. The term "Indian" is firmly established in U.S. law (e.g., the Indian Reorganization Act) and U.S. federal government agencies (e.g., the Bureau of Indian Affairs). Tribes may have their own name for themselves, in their native language, such how the Navajo refer to themselves as Diné, which simply means "the people."

ACKNOWLEDGMENTS

I am grateful to my original dissertation committee, which was comprised of Robert A. Williams Jr., who directed it, Dean Marc L. Miller, and Dr. Raymond D. Austin, three dedicated faculty members and administrators at the University of Arizona James E. Rogers College of Law.

Robert A. Williams Jr. is a world-renowned scholar on the rights of indigenous peoples and critical race theory. He is a dogged fighter for the rights of native people worldwide and for racial justice. I'm grateful to Professor Williams for his lessons on the importance of good, clear writing. I appreciate Professor Williams's interest in my research and career. Professor Williams reminded me to never relent when a case or principle is an important one worth fighting for.

Marc L. Miller is the dean of the law school. His scholarship in the field of criminal procedure, particularly prosecutorial discretion, is widely acclaimed. His support for indigenous legal studies in Tucson is making an impact worldwide.

Dr. Raymond D. Austin has been a source of inspiration for my focus on the customs and traditions of indigenous peoples. His contribution to the integration of custom and tradition into modern tribal law has had a profound impact throughout Indian country in the United States and beyond. Dr. Austin, a former associate justice on the Navajo Nation Supreme Court, was kind enough to share with me sources he unearthed detailing historical Navajo handling of murder cases. I am grateful for his guidance, mentoring, and support. When in doubt throughout this project, I heard his mantra in my head: "Think like an Indian." Although I'm not one, I tried my best to follow his advice. He was distinguished jurist in residence at the University of Arizona College of Law, and today teaches at Northern Arizona University.

Carrie Stussie, formerly at the University of Arizona College of Law Indigenous Peoples Law and Policy Program, provided much logistical help, and Alexandra Delgado was very helpful in library research support. From 2013 to 2014, I was an attorney at the law firm of Cacace, Tusch & Santagata in Stamford, Connecticut, and am grateful to the attorneys and staff there for their support throughout the project. Julie Loehr and Anastasia Wraight at Michigan State University Press are my editors, and I'm grateful for their support and extreme patience.

Finally, I would never have been able to pursue this academic adventure without the day-to-day support of my partner Marian Salzman. Her work with the victims of Newtown, Connecticut, was the light bulb that went off over my head and the beacon that shined the path to my research.

Counting Victims

An Introduction to Indigenous vs. Non-Indigenous Perspectives

O n a cold December morning in 2012, Adam Lanza blasted his way through a locked elementary school and into infamy, shattering a window and the lives of twenty-six families. In many ways Lanza's crime was very similar to that of Jeffrey Weise, a member of the Red Lake Band of Chippewa Indians of Northern Minnesota. Here, I examine how American society reacts to the horrors of mass shootings. I describe insights, ideas, and findings that link rampage shootings and communal responses in the United States and on American Indian reservations, setting the stage for the future study of both the mindset of the shooters and how communities heal in the aftermath.

What happened in Newtown, Connecticut, is so disturbing that a campaign to convince the world it was a hoax garnered mass interest. Self-styled conspiracy theorists, "truthers," claimed essentially that President Barack Obama staged the school shootings at the Sandy Hook Elementary School as a prelude to disarming the U.S. citizenry. They posted videos that immediately went viral on YouTube and were viewed by many millions of viewers.[1]

The truthers captured the imagination of the public, in part, because the reality itself was so disturbing. Twenty-year-old Adam Lanza dressed himself in all black, put on a pair of fingerless gloves, and drove to an elementary school. At 9:30 a.m.,

Lanza, armed with three powerful guns, including a military-style assault rifle and enough bullets to kill hundreds of people, shot his way through the front door and window, bursting into the school. In just ten minutes he killed twenty first graders and six teachers and administrators. His first victim, his mother Nancy Lanza, lay dead in her bed at the family home. Lanza's last shot was to himself, twenty-eight dead in all.

In counting victims, Nancy Lanza was usually excluded. U.S. President Barack Obama set the early example. When the president spoke in Newtown at the memorial service, he said, "We gather here in memory of twenty beautiful children and six remarkable adults," deliberately not counting Nancy Lanza.[2]

President Obama may have been the first to discount Nancy Lanza as a victim, but he was not the last. It is as if the murder did not occur. The University of Connecticut honored the shooting victims with a ceremony before a men's basketball game, with twenty-six students standing at center court holding lighted candles. Officials and victims' family members gathered at the Newtown Town Hall to mark a moment of silence on December 21, 2012. To honor the memory of the victims of the rampage, the bells of the nearby Trinity Episcopal Church were rung twenty-six times, not twenty-seven. In Newtown, the number of victims was always twenty-six.

Nancy Lanza was quietly cremated in Haverhill, Massachusetts. A funeral was held about six months after her death about 180 miles from Newtown in Kingston, New Hampshire. Her sister said Nancy Lanza's family waited to hold the funeral "out of respect for the families of the other victims."[3]

There is a fair amount of evidence that Nancy Lanza was not counted by many as a victim because she was blamed as contributing to the murders or failing to prevent them. The weapons used by Adam Lanza, without exception, were legally purchased over the years by Nancy Lanza.[4] Seven years before the massacre, Adam Lanza was diagnosed with Asperger's disorder and was described as having significant social impairments.[5]

A number of the parents of slain Sandy Hook children very clearly held Nancy Lanza responsible. Nicole Hockley, the mother of six-year-old victim, Dylan Hockley, was one of them. "It's clear that he had mental illness and intervention was not made," she told the *New York Daily News*. "And there was not responsible gun ownership, either." "There was obviously a breakdown in terms of the parenting and the structure in that house," said Bill Sherlach, husband of Sandy Hook Elementary School's slain psychologist Mary Sherlach.[6]

Public opinion in the United States seems to treat Nancy Lanza, "a gun enthusiast who had taught Adam to shoot," as "an accessory to the crime, rather than its victim." Emily Miller, an editor at the *Washington Times*, summed up that sentiment, "We can't blame lax gun-control laws, access to mental health treatment, prescription drugs or video games for Lanza's terrible killing spree. We can point to a mother who should have been more aware of how sick her son had become and forced treatment."[7]

Alissa and Robbie Parker, parents of six-year-old Emilie Parker, a first grader killed at Sandy Hook Elementary School, disagree with the notion that Nancy Lanza was not counted as a victim because she was blamed for the tragedy. According to the Parkers, Nancy Lanza belongs in a separate category of victims than the others. "The reason we (the group of Sandy Hook families) do not address her specifically," said the Parkers, "is that we consider her death a domestic dispute, whereas the number of victims in the mass shooting are those at the school, where the mass shooting took place. Basically, she belongs in the total number of victims by the hands of Adam Lanza, but the number '26 victims' accounts for those that had nothing to do with the Lanza family who lost their lives."[8]

The enormity of the horror of the mass killing of innocent victims causes victims to search for fault, instead of seeking solace. As a result, the parents and family members of the killers often face blame, or extreme hatred for either causing the violence or failing to prevent it. They are even treated as pariahs themselves.

Alissa and Robbie Parker do not think parents of rampagers like Adam Lanza should be treated as pariahs or vilified by society. Alissa Parker said:

> We would like parents to be able to courageously see the struggles their children have and stop at nothing to get them the proper help and treatment without the fear of stigma or backlash from their peers or community. It is important to look at her [Nancy Lanza's] role as Adam's mother and provider to better understand the struggles and obstacles she faced in trying to help Adam as best as she felt she could. Looking at this situation can hopefully help us all learn from those mistakes (not just Nancy's but the "system" as a whole) and progress forward. We feel like placing blame, pointing fingers etc. is an easy way to project our own fears and insecurities onto someone else and not place the responsibility on ourselves.

In the case of Adam Lanza, his body was claimed by his father, Peter Lanza.

What happened after that has been kept a secret by his father, who says nobody will ever figure out what was done with his son's body.[9] There are no reports of a funeral.

The adversarial structure of the American legal system, though, has little room for the healing process necessary after rampage shootings. With the possibility of civil litigation or criminal convictions looming, the legal system encourages the silence of anyone who might have answers. The system protects rights rather than solves problems. The American system of jurisprudence, a form of the Anglo-European system, is a "retributive" system, punishing offenders.[10] It relies upon hierarchies and power, using rank and the coercive power that goes with it to address conflicts.[11]

Many indigenous cultures throughout the world, on the other hand, have long histories of incorporating community healing into their dispute resolution processes. The model employed in select indigenous cultures contrasts the retributive, vertical system. The indigenous model employed in select indigenous communities is referred to as a "horizontal" justice model.[12] This model allows full victim and community participation, treats all participants as equals, and has an end goal of restoring harmony to the community.

For example, dispute resolution among the Maori, the indigenous peoples of New Zealand, illustrates the horizontal model. Before colonization, the Maori convened a *runanga o nga tura*, a council that included elders, representatives of the offenders' family, and representatives of the victims' family.[13] A widely cited example of a modern adaptation practiced by an indigenous culture in North America is that of the Navajo Nation, an indigenous tribe in the southwest of the United States.[14] Today the Navajo Nation's judicial branch runs a program called the Peacemaking Program.[15]

What lessons can we learn from examining select indigenous cultures in North America and their history of emphasis on community participation and healing? Can the indigenous traditions studied provide a formula for approaching the aftermath of modern-day mass shootings when they occur outside of native communities? Where restorative style responses exist in indigenous tradition, how can indigenous traditions of offenders and their families speaking face to face with victims and their families be adapted for modern non-indigenous peoples? What cultural and social barriers exist that make adaptation of the indigenous practices cited less likely?

Rampage Murders

School Shootings in Non-Indigenous Communities

ardly a week seems to pass in the United States without shocking news of a gunman appearing at a school or workplace and opening fire at innocent victims. The term that seems to capture this epidemic is "rampage."[1] A rampage is defined by the fact that it involves an attack on multiple parties, selected almost at random.[2] Sometimes starting out with the idea to kill one or more victims, the killers typically fire off a barrage that kills and maims many. These attacks usually target whole institutions such as schools or workplaces rather than individuals. In most instances the killer does not know their victims or have any relationship with them.

A rampage is a mass murder. Sometimes the term is used interchangeably with the terms "serial murder," "spree murder," or more recently, "rampage murder," as are the phrases "mass murder" or "mass killing."[3] Mass murder is a single episodic act of violence occurring at one time and in one place. The number of victims required to classify a shooting as a mass murder varies.[4] Indeed, some authorities have set the number at three victims, while others have defined it as four victims.[5] For purposes of this book, for the most part, I exclude political killings, acts of warfare or terrorism, and killings committed by more than two perpetrators. Sometimes, however, as in the 2016 Orlando nightclub massacre, it's virtually impossible to rule out political or terrorist motivations. The term "shooting" is used where appropriate, as guns are the primary weapon in most of these incidents. When the incident occurred at a school, a common but not universal theme, the term is applied. A list of mass shootings (all categories) in the United States over the last thirty-six years (1982–2018) is included in appendix 2.[6]

In most instances, killers do not know their victims. The less of a relationship the killer has with his victims, the more likely the victims are free of any ill-will toward the killer. Recent cases such as Stephen Paddock in Las Vegas, Nevada; Jared Loughner in Tucson, Arizona; James Holmes in Aurora, Colorado; Dylann Roof in Charleston, South Carolina; and Omar Mateen in Orlando, Florida, are all cases of shooters who had no relationship with their victims. For the country as a whole, these shootings forced the kind of searching self-examination that comes from a total shock.[7]

Rampages pose more questions than answers. Americans struggle to determine what causes tragic rampages and why they seem to occur with such great frequency. Are we no longer able to keep ourselves and our children safe in our communities? Are schools, movie theaters, shopping malls, and churches no longer inviolable? Is there now more mental illness than used to exist and is it going untreated? Are powerful weapons so commonplace that we are no longer surprised when they are used to mow down innocent people? Were there warning signs exhibited by the killers that were ignored?

So often with rampage killing, society itself is the target. The school, the factory, the church itself is where the rage is focused. Pain and hurt is felt across the greater community. It is felt nationally or even internationally.

Having defined the terms I will use, I now turn to a discussion of the adversarial structure of the American legal system, a system that leaves little room for the healing process necessary after rampage murders. Before assessing the aftermath, I will review exactly what transpired in three recent and well-known school rampages in the United States.

Columbine High School, Jefferson County, Colorado

The 1999 rampage in Colorado is so well known, it is referred to with one word: "Columbine." Moreover, it is a word that evokes strong reaction. In contrast, Eric Harris and Dylan Klebold used two words; they called it "Judgment Day."[8] As a result of live television coverage, the world witnessed the April 20, 1999, Columbine High School shootings in real time. The images were shocking.

Columbine High School is located in Jefferson County, Colorado. Although it is typically reported as being in Littleton, Colorado, the school actually sits about a mile outside the city limits and is part of the Jefferson County public school system.

Without ever alerting their parents, teachers, friends, or the local police, for nearly two years high school students Eric Harris, eighteen, and Dylan Klebold, seventeen, plotted and schemed murderous mayhem.[9] They barely hid their intentions; in their bedroom closets they assembled a vast arsenal of guns and bombs.

Harris and Klebold planned a military-style attack designed to "outdo" Timothy McVeigh, the man who killed 168 people in the Oklahoma City bombing of the Murrah Federal Building in 1995.[10] If their scheme had worked as planned, the two would have achieved their objective: many hundreds would have died. Their bombs were made with typical barbeque-grill propane tanks easily purchased by the general public at any supermarket in America, and other ingredients.[11] Harris found the design for the bombs on a website, the Anarchist Cookbook.[12] The propane tanks weighed twenty pounds each and were obtained by Harris and Klebold in their neighborhood. One design of bombs used an aerosol can as a detonator wired to a nostalgic alarm clock used as a timer, including the old-fashioned bell on top. The propane tanks were connected to gasoline cans, nails, and BBs, which were attached as shrapnel.

The nightmarish scheme had several phases. The first phase was to detonate two "decoy" bombs in a neighborhood park to draw police away from the high school.[13] Klebold and Harris would then nonchalantly walk into the school lugging heavy duffel bags filled with the propane and gasoline bombs. The plan was for one set of bombs to be placed in the school outdoor commons, which would be filled with students. The other set of bombs was intended to explode in the school cafeteria at a time when it was filled with students eating lunch.

The boys planned to use the two sets of bombs to set the school in a fiery blaze and instill mass confusion and chaos. More strategically, the bombs were intended to send students and teachers fleeing for the exits and the parking lots. With macabre precision, Harris and Klebold planned to place themselves in two strategic locations in the parking lot—at two of the three main school exits, armed with powerful guns to literally mow down fellow high school students and adults as they came running out through the doors.

Harris and Klebold planned to gear up in infantry-style clothing, with web harnessing to allow them to attach ammunition and explosives to their bodies. They planned to use two guns apiece. Dylan Klebold used an Intratec TEC-DC9 semiautomatic handgun and a shotgun to do his shooting. Eric Harris used a Hi-Point 9mm carbine rifle and a shotgun.[14] Each killer was carrying a backpack and duffel bag, and in addition they each carried in some eighty pounds of explosives, including pipe bombs and Molotov cocktail–style bombs. On the morning of April 20, 1999, Klebold and Harris left their homes, their parents having no idea what mayhem their children had conceived for that infamous day.

Fortunately for the students and teachers of Columbine High School, not one of the homemade bombs and detonators worked as planned. First, the decoy bombs in the park only partially detonated, producing a bang and a grass fire, not the ball of fire and smoke envisioned by the two conspirators.[15] The boys entered the crowded school and placed the bomb-laden duffle bags in the commons and cafeteria as planned. They nonchalantly walked past hundreds of students, faculty, and staff while setting down the deadly bombs. Videotapes of the incident do not reveal that anyone noticed anything awry. Harris and Klebold went to their two cars in the parking lot and suited up as planned, strapping guns to their bodies.

When the sets of propane and gasoline bombs in the commons and cafeteria did not go off as planned, Harris and Klebold came together outside in the parking lot and grabbed their guns. Outside, students were picnicking, or exiting the school doors. Harris and Klebold started shooting at the students outside and throwing pipe bombs in their direction. At that time two students were killed outside.[16]

Harris and Klebold then went into the school, walking through the halls. Their spree is captured on surveillance cameras. Harris and Klebold next shot students in the cafeteria and the library, throwing pipe bombs down the halls. They killed ten students in the library.[17] Police and television station camera crews flocked to the high school, and within twenty-eight minutes television stations went live with the scene of the mayhem. Shockingly, students who remained in classrooms actually watched the live coverage on classroom televisions. Inside, fires were burning, fire alarms were ringing, and sprinklers were spraying water. It was a war zone.

The world watched on television as Patrick Ireland, a severely wounded and partially paralyzed seventeen-year-old student, managed to climb out of a classroom window. CNN spoke live to another student on his cell phone as he described the scene inside—all while Harris and Klebold continued their assault.[18] Bodies lay dead or wounded outside and throughout the school building while hundreds of students hid in classrooms and closets. Police begged the television stations to stop broadcasting the scene. As students flocked out of the school in horror, they were interviewed on television, and many were eager to speak. Reunions with parents, too, were broadcast live.

Harris and Klebold did not die in a shoot-out with police, or even at the last second before being captured. All alone in a quiet spot in the library, Harris and Klebold used their own guns to commit suicide with self-inflicted fatal shots to their heads. It was three hours before police found their bodies.[19]

Police processed the interior of the school as a bomb scene for an entire day, surrounding the perimeter of the school in police tape. Names of deceased students were not released to parents. During this day of unimaginable terror, parents of missing children were given no information. Bodies lay dead outside and inside the school. One boy, Danny Rohrbough, fifteen, lay dead on the sidewalk in a pool of blood for twenty-eight hours. His dead body was visible to the public and to the news media. A friend telephoned the boy's father and warned him that there was a photo in the morning *Rocky Morning News* of a boy lying "motionless" in a pool of blood on the sidewalk.[20]

In all, thirteen were killed by Harris and Klebold, twelve students and one teacher.[21] The two suicides of the killers made the death toll fifteen.[22] (A list of the victims killed at Columbine High School is included in appendix 1.) Twenty-four students were wounded, several permanently disabled.[23] The live viewing on television of this horrific spectacle caused shockwaves throughout the world. Whether the stereotype is fitting or not, Littleton, Colorado, appeared to Americans to be the last place they would expect to witness mass murder. As such, Columbine became a tremendous media story. It was the number one story of 1999 on CNN and the seventh highest media event of the 1990s.[24] Sixty-eight percent of Americans closely followed the Columbine news story.

The dramatic nature of the events of Columbine led to the high level of media coverage of the tragedy. It became a "defining event" for journalists.[25] Journalists had never experienced an event like Columbine before. Further, it came to symbolize the school shooting crisis, and to a lesser extent, the juvenile crime problem as a whole.[26]

With its vast media coverage and influence, it is not surprising that Columbine has played an important role in influencing the school shootings that followed it. In September 2006 Brian Draper and Torey Adamcik killed Cassie Jo Stoddart in Boise, Idaho. Draper was obsessed with Columbine and he and Adamcik warned people that they were going to commit a "Columbine-like" school shooting.[27] In a videotape mailed to NBC News, Seung-Hui Cho, the Virginia Tech college student who killed thirty-two people in 2007, referred to Klebold and Harris as "martyrs."[28] The official report of the state's attorney investigating the Sandy Hook Elementary School murders reports that Adam Lanza "had an obsession with mass murders, in particular the April 1999 shootings at Columbine High School in Colorado."[29]

In April 2014, a copycat scheme was discovered and foiled in Minnesota, planned to coincide with the fifteenth anniversary of Columbine. John LaDue, a seventeen-year-old high school student in Waseca, Minnesota, stockpiled guns and bomb-making materials at his home and at a storage facility. Like Klebold and Harris, he planned a decoy event to distract police, and like them, he planned to detonate bombs in the cafeteria at his high school.[30] A neighbor who observed him walking through her yard with large bags called police. Authorities arrested LaDue before he could stage his Columbine-like tragedy.

Virginia Tech, Blacksburg, Virginia

Virginia Tech is a state university located in the town of Blacksburg, Virginia.[31] Blacksburg is located in Montgomery County in the New River Valley and is thirty-eight miles southwest of Roanoke. The university is a historic land-grant institution that currently enrolls about 30,000 students on a sprawling 2,600-acre campus of 135 buildings.[32]

Seung-Hui Cho, born in Seoul, South Korea, moved with his family to Maryland in 1992. As early as 1999, as an eight-year-old middle school student, teachers noted suicidal and homicidal ideations in his school writings and in his references to Columbine.[33] Cho entered Virginia Tech in 2003 as a business information systems major. In 2005 problems begin to surface and an English professor noted a concern about a trend of violence in his writing. Numerous complaints were made about him from females. Cho was treated for mental health in 2005 and 2006. In the spring of 2006, Cho wrote a paper for a creative writing class about a student who hated his fellow students and planned to kill the students and himself.

From February to April 2007, Cho, then twenty-three and an English major, purchased numerous guns and ammunition. He ordered online a .22-caliber Walther P22 handgun and picked it up later at a pawn shop across the street from the university. He bought a 9mm Glock-19 handgun at Roanoke Firearms. He purchased the ammunition for the guns at Walmart, Dicks Sporting Goods, and on eBay.[34] Cho planned his rampage and assembled a package intended for the news media. In the package were photographs of Cho holding guns, an 1,800 word "diatribe," and videotaped material of him expressing his rage, resentment, and desire to get even with his "oppressors."[35]

Cho committed his murders in the early morning hours of April 16, 2007, moving from a dormitory residence to classrooms in the engineering building. He started at about 7:00 a.m. at the West Ambler Johnston residence hall where he shot student Emily Hilscher in her dorm room.[36] A residential assistant (RA), Ryan Clark, whose room was next door, likely came to investigate the noise. Cho shot him next, and he died from the gunshot. The *Wall Street Journal* reported that Hilscher died three hours after the shooting and that her family was not notified of her shooting until after she died.[37] There are no known links between Hilscher and Cho.[38]

Cho next went to the Blacksburg post office where he mailed the media package to NBC News in New York. It arrived at NBC the next day. Cho then walked to Norris Hall, an engineering building. In a backpack he carried a stash of guns, a knife, a hammer, and four hundred rounds of ammunition in a backpack. Using chains he bought at Home Depot, Cho chained shut (from the inside) the three main doors of the building.

Cho next entered a classroom in Norris Hall where a small graduate engineering class, Advanced Hydrology, was taking place. There were just thirteen students in the class. Cho shot and killed the professor, then shot at the students.[39] Cho then moved across the hall and entered another classroom where an elementary German class was taking place. He shot the teacher and then shot at the students. Cho next moved down the hall and entered a French class. Cho walked down one row of the classroom and shot at the students and the teacher.

Cho next returned to the German class, trying unsuccessfully to get back into the room but students were able to barricade him from entering. He went back to the French class, shooting again at the teacher and several of the students. Eleven students and the teacher died in that classroom.[40] Six surviving students in that classroom suffered gunshot wounds. Cho next tried to enter a classroom where a mechanics class was being taught by seventy-six-year-old professor Liviu Librescu. Librescu barricaded Cho from entering by bracing his body against the door, yelling to students to jump out of the window. Cho shot through the door, killing Librescu through the door. Most of Librescu's students escaped out of the classroom window. Cho shot at two students as they attempted to escape through the window.[41]

Librescu's students later viewed him as a hero. He never gave up on trying to keep Cho out of his classroom. When Librescu succumbed to a fatal shot in the head, Cho made his way into the room. The irony of Librescu's life was that as a Jew he survived a Nazi labor camp in Romania, only to succumb to a school-shooting rampage in the United States.[42]

After Librescu's mechanics classroom, Cho then returned to the hydrology class and shot more students there. In total he killed nine of the thirteen students in that classroom and wounded three more. Police managed to blast their way into Norris Hall and proceeded to the second floor where they heard the sounds of the mayhem. Just as the police reached the second floor, Cho, in the French classroom, fatally shot himself in the head.

Cho's shooting spree in Norris Hall took just eleven minutes. During the eleven minutes he fired 174 rounds, killed thirty people and himself, and wounded another seventeen.[43] Counting the two students he killed at the dormitory, he murdered a total of thirty-two; he was the thirty-third. Five of the fatalities were faculty members and twenty-seven were students. In addition to the seventeen students wounded by gunfire, another six were injured jumping out of second-floor classrooms.[44] (A list of the victims killed at Virginia Tech is included in appendix 1.)

While there are mass murders in history with more fatalities, more casualties were suffered in the Virginia Tech rampage than any other school shooting in history. As with Columbine, there were many missed warning signs about Cho, his violent writings, the stalking complaints made against him, and his mental health history. After Virginia Tech, the school shooting with the highest casualty toll is the 2012 rampage in Newtown, Connecticut. Newtown is the second-most catastrophic school shooting in history and the most catastrophic in a high school or grade school.

Sandy Hook Elementary School, Newtown, Connecticut

Sandy Hook is a historic community located within the town of Newtown, Connecticut. Newtown is located at the northern end of Fairfield County, about equidistant (approximately forty-five miles) from New York City and Hartford, Connecticut. Newtown is a racially and socially homogenous, mainstream, and affluent suburban community. Sometime early on the morning of December 14, 2012, Adam Lanza, age twenty, shot and killed his mother, Nancy Lanza, who was sleeping in bed in the family home in Newtown. He used a .22-caliber Savage Mark II rifle and shot her twice in the head.[45]

At around 9:30 a.m. Lanza drove his Honda Civic to the Sandy Hook Elementary School in Newtown. He was suited up mostly in black, including black fingerless gloves. He put earplugs in both ears. Lanza parked his car in front of the school and then approached the entrance armed with three guns—a Bushmaster Model XM 15-E2S rifle, a Glock 20 10mm handgun, a Sig Sauer P226 handgun—and hundreds of rounds of live ammunition.[46] A fourth gun, an Izhmash Saiga-12 shotgun, was found in his car.

The front door of the school was locked, but Lanza blasted his way into the school building, blowing out plate glass windows next to the front door. When the first shots rang out, the school principal Dawn Hochsprung, forty-seven, and school psychologist Mary Sherlach, fifty-six, were in a meeting. Hearing the gunshots, the two women ran down the hall to investigate. With the rifle, Lanza shot and killed both of the women.[47] Lanza shot at other staff members in the hallway, wounding two.[48] He next turned his attention to the classrooms. He entered two first-grade classrooms. One classroom was being taught by a substitute teacher, thirty-year-old Lauren Rousseau, and twenty-nine-year-old behavioral therapist Rachel Davino. Lanza shot and killed both adults and fifteen first grade students in that classroom.

In the other first-grade classroom were twenty-seven-year-old teacher Victoria Soto and fifty-two-year-old teacher Anne Marie Murphy. Lanza shot and killed both women.[49] Five of the children belonging in that classroom were found by police, four having died of gunshot wounds. The fifth died at the hospital.[50] Nine children ran out of Soto's classroom and two hid in the bathroom. At 9:40 a.m. Lanza committed suicide in that classroom by firing one fatal shot to his head with the Glock 20 10mm handgun.[51]

In the other classrooms and offices, students, teachers, and staff members hid in classroom bathrooms and closets wherever they could find them. The school librarian, Yvonne Cech, for example, locked herself along with another staff person and eighteen fourth graders in a closet behind file cabinets while listening to the disturbing sounds of the gunshots. They hid there for forty-five nightmarish minutes until a police SWAT team arrived and escorted them out of the closet and out of the building. Police officers led children past the carnage of blood and dead students, teachers, and staff members. The police told the children to "close your eyes, hold hands," according to nine-year-old Vanessa Bajraliu.[52]

"Carnage" suitably describes the scene. Lanza fired many rounds at each victim. Wayne Carver, the chief medical examiner said that every casualty was struck more than once, and some as many as eleven times. "This is a very devastating set of injuries," Carver said.[53]

Lanza's rampage lasted just ten minutes. At the school he killed twenty children and six adults (teachers and staff members) before killing himself. Adding his mother and himself, there were twenty-eight fatalities. Two adult staff members were wounded. Seventeen of the children were just six years old and three were seven years old.[54] (A list of the victims killed by Lanza in Newtown is included in appendix 1.)

Surviving children were taken to the nearby Sandy Hook Volunteer Fire and Rescue Station House. There were many joyous reunions at the firehouse, as parents arrived after having flocked to the school from wherever they were. Meanwhile, in the same firehouse, twenty families began to grasp the reality that they would never speak to their children again. Those parents were ushered into a separate, somber room.

Lanza's targets—first graders—set him apart from other rampage killers. The faces of twenty dead children, twelve innocent little girls and eight innocent little boys, tore open a raw and exposed nerve across the world. The children were referred to as babies. "I've been here for eleven years," said Laura Feinstein, a reading support teacher at Sandy Hook who survived the rampage. "I can't imagine who would do this to our poor little babies."[55]

American suburban communities like Newtown, Connecticut, and Littleton, Colorado, are settings easily recognizable to many people. Similarly, Virginia Tech, as a college campus provides a recognizable setting. Having examined in great detail three school rampage murder cases occurring in settings understood by many, the next chapter examines rampages occurring in a less familiar setting, namely American Indian reservations.

When Mass Shootings Occur on American Indian Reservations

Studies in Contrast

Before delving into an analysis of rampage murders on Indian reservations or those affecting indigenous peoples in North America, I will review the demographics of the American Indian population. According to the most recent count (2010 U.S. Census data), there are more than five million American Indian/Alaskan Natives in the United States. This number includes 2.9 million people who identify themselves as either American Indian/Alaskan Native plus another 2.3 million people who identify themselves as American Indian/Alaskan Native in combination with another race. These five million people represent 1.7 percent of the total American population.

There are 566 federally recognized Indian nations in the United States. They are ethnically, culturally, and linguistically diverse and are sometimes called "tribes," "bands," "nations," "pueblos," "communities," and "native villages." In addition to the federally recognized nations, there are also nations recognized by individual state governments. The 2010 census identified six tribal groupings, or nations, with populations of more than one hundred thousand: Cherokee, Navajo, Choctaw, Mexican American Indian, Chippewa, Sioux, Apache, and Blackfeet.[1]

According to the 2010 census forty-one percent of American Indians live in the western region of the United States. The state of California accounts for the largest number of American Indians of any state, followed by Oklahoma, Arizona, Texas, and New York. American Indians are younger than the non-native population. About one-third of American Indians are under eighteen compared to about one-quarter for the overall population. As of 2017 the median age for American Indians is thirty-three compared to thirty-eight for the overall U.S. population.[2]

American Indians face many economic, health, and political challenges. Nearly one-third of natives live in poverty, and this number is higher when counting the natives who live on a reservation. Nonetheless, American Indians are making economic progress. The number of American Indian–owned businesses has increased. In 2007 total receipts of the native-owned businesses were $34.5 billion, up 28.3 percent from 2002. In the decade from 1990 to 2000, income levels rose by 33 percent and the poverty rate dropped by 7 percent.

Gaming enterprises are a significant part of American Indian economies. By 2010, the majority of American Indian tribes were considered "gaming tribes." States that permit Indian gaming have come to heavily rely on the whopping $1.4 billion that tribal gaming contributes to state tax revenues. It is estimated that more than nine in ten American Indians reside on reservations with gaming enterprises.

Indian tribes possess nearly one quarter of the U.S. onshore oil and gas reserves and developable resources and one-third of the low-sulfur coal produced in the American West. Today, however, they represent less than 5 percent of current national energy production. On a positive note, the number of native students enrolled in colleges and universities, and the number of postsecondary degrees awarded to natives, has more than doubled in the past thirty years.

Natives are much more likely to die of the following causes than non-natives: tuberculosis, alcoholism, diabetes, motor vehicle crashes, injury, and suicide. In fact, Indian youth have the highest rate of suicide among all ethnic groups in the United States, and suicide is the second-leading cause of death for native youth aged fifteen to twenty-four. The school shooting at Red Lake High School was one such native youth suicide.

The Red Lake Band of Chippewa Indians is an American Indian tribe with a reservation (Red Lake Reservation) located on a vast expanse of land and water, nearly eight hundred thousand acres in Northern Minnesota.[3] There are four reservation communities in this area: Little Rock, Ponemah, Redby, and Red Lake.[4] The tribe is governed by an eleven-member tribal council. Seven hereditary chiefs serve for life in an advisory capacity. These seven chiefs are descendants of the leaders who negotiated land agreements with the United States in 1889 and who resisted the allotment of the Dawes Allotment Act of 1887; as a result, all Red Lake land is now held in common by all tribal members.[5] As such, the Red Lake Reservation is referred to as a "closed" reservation and very few non-members live there.[6]

The Red Lake Tribe refused efforts to join together with other Minnesota tribes, refusing, in 1934, to join together with six other Chippewa bands.[7] The Red Lake Band has persevered to preserve the Anishinaabe heritage and tradition. The Ojibwe language is the first language of many tribal members.[8]

Tragedy Strikes the Red Lake Reservation

Sixteen-year-old Jeffrey Weise, a Red Lake Chippewa Indian, lived with his grandmother, Shelda Lussier. He had been suspended from Red Lake High School and was being tutored at home by a visiting teacher.[9] Weise's mother lived in a nursing home in another city and suffered from brain damage resulting from an auto accident.[10] Weise's father committed suicide years before.

On the morning of March 21, 2005, Weise went to his grandfather's home. His grandfather, Daryl Lussier, fifty-nine, was a thirty-year veteran of the Red Lake Tribal Police Department who reached the rank of sergeant. With a .22-caliber pistol, Weise shot and killed his grandfather along with his grandfather's thirty-one-year-old girlfriend, Michelle Sigana, as they both lay in bed asleep.[11] Weise searched his grandfather's home for more weapons. He grabbed a 12-gauge shotgun from the house, a .44-caliber automatic pistol and ammunition. He loaded the two guns and drove his grandfather's tribal police cruiser to Red Lake High School, located on the reservation.

Weise drove up to the front of the school and parked directly in front of the main entrance.[12] Dressed in all black he walked out of the car and very casually walked into the school. He held the shotgun close to his side, muzzle pointed to the ground. Without hesitation Weise walked straight through the front entrance metal detectors. The metal detectors were attended by two unarmed uniformed security officers, Derrick Brun and an unidentified female guard.

Without flinching or hesitating, Weise shot and killed the twenty-eight-year-old Brun.[13] He fired a shot down the hallway, almost hitting Neva Rogers, a teacher.[14] She ran down the school hallway to alert teachers and students of what was happening, rushing into a classroom occupied by a ninth-grade study hall.[15] As people began to comprehend what was occurring, teachers locked classroom doors and hid with students behind bookcases and desks.[16]

Weise walked through the school in what is described as a "cool," "calm" and "collected" manner.[17] He didn't run.[18] He kicked out glass from classroom doors, stepped into a classroom, and shot at the students and teachers gathered on the floor and under desks.[19]

Ninth grader Jeffrey May, sitting in the study hall, flipped a table on its side, crouching behind it with classmates. Weise blasted his way into the classroom. "God save us," pleaded the teacher, Neva Rogers. Weise shot her in the head, killing her. He then turned his attention on the students huddled in the back of the room. "Do you guys believe in God?" he asked. One boy said no. Weise started shooting, killing five students. He tried to shoot the teacher, Missy Dodds, but the gun was empty.[20]

Weise went to reload. May, a six-foot-tall, 250-pound varsity football player, lunged at Weise as he was reloading, and tried to stab Weise with a pencil, but Weise was wearing a protective vest. They wrestled. Weise shot May in the face with a pistol. The bullet entered his cheek below his right eye, fractured his jaw, and lodged in his neck.[21]

Weise went into several classrooms at least twice, killing and wounding students and teachers both times. The classrooms he entered more than once were the rooms where he did the most harm.[22]

Four Red Lake tribal police officers rushed to the school and moved quickly. Rather than wait for a tactical team to arrive, they decided to enter.[23] Once inside the officers located Weise and shot at him.[24] Weise ran back into the classroom where most of his victims lay dead, and holding his grandfather's shotgun to his head, he pulled the trigger. He died instantly.

Missy Dodds and many students in her study hall classroom credit Jeffrey May with saving their lives. May was airlifted to a hospital over one hundred miles away in Fargo, North Dakota. He suffered a stroke that immobilized his left side. The bullet in his neck was surgically removed. May survived and went through a lengthy rehabilitation.[25]

In addition to Daryl Lussier, Michelle Sigana (Lussier's girlfriend), Derrick Brun (the security guard), five students, and one teacher were killed by Weise. (A list of the victims killed at Red Lake High School is included in appendix 1.) Including Weise, ten people died at Red Lake High School on March 21, 2005. Five students were treated for wounds at two hospitals and two students received head wounds that required specialized surgery.[26]

The Aftermath of the Red Lake Tragedy

There were many obvious similarities between the Red Lake tragedy and Columbine. In both cases, teenage boys dressed in all black, who claimed to follow and admire Adolph Hitler, acted out fantasies, committed mass killings at a school, and then ended the massacre by killing themselves.[27]Although many people focused on Jeffrey Weise and what might have led him to the murders at Red Lake, the response from the tribal community differed significantly from response to other mass killings presented in the previous chapter that did not involve American Indian communities.

On the Red Lake Reservation, there was very little public anger toward Weise or talk of revenge.[28] There was no talk of filing lawsuits against the Red Lake Tribe or others. "That's not our way," said Brenda Child, a historian at the University of Minnesota who grew up on the Red Lake Reservation.[29] "We're all one community. It's an Indian thing. It's different than a suburb of Denver. We have a long history together in this particular place. Since it's your own extended family suffering in the aftermath of this, people are feeling a lot of sympathy.... It makes our relationships deeper and more complicated."[30]

Another example of unusual compassion and a surprising lack of bitterness at Red Lake was that of Jodi May, Jeffrey May's mother. Jodi May knew Weise's grandparents; in fact, his grandmother helped raise her when she was a child. With the existence of these family ties on the reservation, it is understandable that Jodi May held no bitterness toward Weise:

> I have a lot of things going on in my mind about the shooter. But, that was when it first happened. I can't really say for anybody else, but it happened—we can't take it back. If he [Jeffrey Weise] was a loner, and to my knowledge my boys were his friends I don't know. I don't have no grudge against nobody, I just want my son to get better.[31]

Jeffrey May remained in the hospital for more than a year, including time spent on difficult physical rehabilitation. He could speak, but with a slight slur. He limped and his left arm was paralyzed.[32]

Memorials and Funerals

Red Lake tribal members began collecting bundles of sage to be given as gifts and burned during funeral ceremonies.[33] They assembled blankets and toys to be placed in caskets. A private memorial service was held on the Wednesday following the tragedy.[34]

Like Columbine, the Red Lake tragedy also mirrors the Sandy Hook Elementary School tragedy in many ways. Adam Lanza accessed guns from his mother, Nancy Lanza, before he murdered her. Weise accessed one of the guns he used from his grandfather, Daryl Lussier, before murdering him. Yet the community, the surviving victims, and the victims' families did not blame Lussier for the murders.

Lussier's family had no difficulty arranging a memorial or funeral for Lussier. He was one of the first to be buried, and a memorial service was held for him at the tribe's own humanities building. At the memorial service for Lussier, there was singing and a drum circle.[35] Lussier was given a dignified burial. He was allowed to be dressed in his police uniform, an eagle feather was placed in his hands, and an American flag was placed in his casket.[36] More than one hundred police officers attended the five-hour funeral for Lussier, which was also attended by U.S. senator Norm Coleman and Minnesota governor Tim Pawlenty, who spoke at the funeral.[37]

Publicly, Lussier was spoken about reverentially. He was referred to by his nickname, "Dash."[38] "If you knew him, you said Dash, and everyone knew who you were talking about," said Ed Naranjo, a retired Bureau of Indian Affairs official who worked with Lussier. "He was that kind of individual who could calm a very hot situation," said Naranjo.[39]

Other more traditional Indian funerals followed for three of the victims from the town of Ponemah, which is on the north side of the Red Lake Reservation.[40] Those funerals, conducted in the Ojibwe language by the victims' families and a tribal spiritual leader, typically lasted two nights and three days, and featured food, pipe ceremonies, and the burning of sage. At Red Lake they conducted the same ceremonies practiced long before the arrival of the Europeans.[41]

The spiritual leader conducting the ceremonies in Ponemah was likely Thomas Stillday Jr. Speaking in general terms about the Red Lake funeral ceremonies for the Red Lake victims, Stillday said: "Our traditional funerals, we talk about God, the creator and all his helpers. We talk about the Holy Ghost and all his helpers. These are the things we talk about in ceremony, to show these kids' souls when they go to the spiritual world."[42]

The Community's Treatment of Jeffrey Weise

While the treatment of Daryl Lussier stands in contrast to that of Nancy Lanza, it is the community's treatment of Jeffrey Weise that is most noteworthy. The family of Jeffrey Weise did not have any difficulty finding a place to hold his funeral or a place to bury him. Minutes after the funeral for Derrick Brun concluded at St. Mary's Catholic Mission, the church filled up again for the funeral of Weise.[43] Weise was given a church funeral. This is extremely unusual for a rampager. Weise's family asked news media to leave the church during the service. The service for Weise drew a somber and large crowd of several hundred people.[44]

One person who attended Weise's funeral said she was ready to forgive Weise. Her comments are illuminating: "He was also a member of Red Lake and he was also somebody's son, brother, uncle," said Kim Baker. "And the way I look at it, he still deserves some recognition from the community so he can't be forgotten."[45] Patrick Defoe, who lost five relatives in the shooting, said: "I've forgiven him. That's a step. That's a first step: forgiving. . . . There are circumstances that led up to this and we don't know, we'll never know."[46] Jodi May, the mother of Jeffrey May, wounded by Weise, was sympathetic to Weise. "The way I think of it, you know, he was a victim before this happened. Nobody reached out to help him."[47]

The Red Lake Tribe Awards Weise's Family Compensation

Without delay, in the days following the Red Lake tragedy, several memorial accounts were created to support the victims and their families with money raised from a number of sources. Funds were created at Wells Fargo Bank, along with the Red Lake National Memorial Fund, Red Lake School Tragedy Assistance Fund, and the Victims' Families of Red Lake Memorial Fund. The Blandin Foundation, a nonprofit organization, granted $250,000 for the youth at Red Lake. Later on, Minnesota state resources were obtained to help Red Lake get "back on its physical and emotional feet."[48] Further, $455,000 coming from restitution funds from a white-collar fraud case was awarded to remodel the high school.

From one memorial fund of $200,000, the Red Lake Tribal Council distributed $5,000 to the families of fifteen victims.[49] In doing so, however, the Red Lake Tribe did something extremely unusual in mass killings: they voted to award the family of the perpetrator $5,000 in victim's aid.[50] Red Lake Tribal Secretary Judy Roy said that the tribal council decided unanimously that Weise should be considered a victim, and that his family should get help paying for his funeral and burial.[51] Roy said of the $5,000, "It's not for him, it's for the family . . . they have a double burden."

Family members of other victims were not unanimous in their support of the tribal council's action. Donna Lewis, the mother of Dewayne Lewis, was outraged. Her son, fifteen, was a student killed by Weise at the high school. As the council debated the award for Weise, she stormed out of the meeting. "He ain't no victim in this. . . . He was a murderer," she said.[52] She also was quoted as attributing some blame to Weise's family: the family "knew he was having problems," and should have helped him.[53] The family member of another murdered victim was also critical of the tribal award. Victoria Brun, the sister of murdered security guard Derrick Brun, asked, "Why are they considering him to be a victim when he killed everybody? . . . The people who donated the money have a right to know and question how the money is divided."[54]

Weise's family received a second award from a small private fund managed by a Red Lake tribal member and distant relative of Weise, Wanda Parkhurst. Parkhurst included Weise's family in the nearly $1,500 she raised and distributed. The *Los Angeles Times* said Parkhurst considered Weise a victim who hurt people because he was under the influence of the neo-Nazi websites he visited and because he was picked on.[55] Referring to the families of Weise's victims, she said, "Those families have a right to hate, but they also have to look at what caused it."[56]

Red Lake and Tragedy in Indian Country: Some Inherent Differences

There are numerous distinctions that contribute to an aftermath at Red Lake that sets it apart from rampage killings among non-indigenous peoples. Kim Baker's remarks, quoted above, reflect the close family ties that Indian people, today, still possess. She saw Weise as belonging to the Red Lake community. It was significant to her that he was tied to the community through his relatives. Like others on the Red Lake Reservation, she refused to turn her back on Weise or his family.

Family relationships are of utmost importance to American Indians who live traditional, less assimilated lives. The Navajo (Diné), for example, a large American Indian tribe in the southwest of the United States, have values that are reinforced through a sophisticated clan system.[57] Navajo traditions reflect that family relationships are indispensable. For the Red Lake Nation, families, too, are tied together in clans, seven of them: bear, turtle, bullhead, eagle, kingfisher, pine marten, and mink.[58]

With 95 percent of its residents being tribal members, Red Lake Reservation is distinguished from other American Indian reservations. Many other reservations include within their population a larger number of non-tribal members. The non-tribal members might be spouses or domestic partners of tribal members. This unusual aspect of the Red Lake Reservation, no doubt, also contributed to the community response to the tragedy.

Tragedy Strikes Several Native American Communities in 2014

Until the shooting on the Red Lake Reservation, there had not been a widely reported rampage shooting involving American Indian people. In the last few years it has become apparent that Jeffrey Weise was not the lone, aberrational Native American rampage offender. Within a span of eight months in 2014, three mass shootings occurred involving Indians.

Marysville Pilchuck High School, Marysville, Washington

A tragedy occurred on October 24, 2014, in Marysville, Washington. Local police released reports detailing how fifteen-year-old Marysville Pilchuck High School student Jaylen Fryberg shot and killed four fellow students in the high school cafeteria before using the gun to commit suicide.[59] Two others were injured. Fryberg himself was the fifth to die.

Fryberg was a member of the Tulalip Indian Tribes of Washington State; he and many of his victims were associated with the tribe and the Muckleshoot Reservation.[60] The school was not located on the reservation but was a short distance from it.

Fryberg first sent text messages asking several of his friends and cousins to meet him in the school cafeteria. Fryberg arrived in the cafeteria and shot six students with a .40-caliber Beretta handgun.[61] Fryberg's victims were fourteen-year-olds Shaylee Chuckulnaskit, Zoe Raine Galasso, and Gia Soriano and Fryberg's fifteen-year-old cousin Andrew Fryberg.[62] Fryberg's other cousin, Nate Hatch, fourteen, was shot in the jaw but survived, enduring surgeries to repair his jaw.[63] The weapon used by Fryberg was registered to Fryberg's father, Raymond Fryberg, and was owned illegally.[64] Fryberg's motive was not clear, but he recently broke up with his girlfriend and was distraught over it.[65]

Michelle Galasso, the mother of victim Zoe Galasso, spoke of a visit she had with Jaylen Fryberg's mother after the rampage. The two mothers embraced, and Galasso said she told Mrs. Fryberg, "I love you."[66] Galasso did not blame the parents of Fryberg and treated them as fellow grieving parents. Of Jaylen's mother, Galasso said, "She's hurting. She's grieving. She lost her child as well."[67] Galasso also said: "In order for me to heal from this, I have to forgive because I cannot waste my life hating or being angry. I just can't. . . . I'll never know why he did it and he took away one of the best things that I ever brought into this world, but he's a child too."[68]

Fryberg's cousin, Keryn Parks, survived the massacre, jumping under a cafeteria table as Fryberg started shooting. A year after the murders she forgave Fryberg: "I forgive him. He's my family. He's my blood."[69] The high school left pictures of Fryberg in the school yearbook, and students included him in collages made of victims' photographs.[70]

Just as the Red Lake Chippewa Indian community supported the family of Jeffrey Weise, the Tulalip Tribes of Washington supported the family of Jaylen Fryberg. While denouncing his murderous actions, tribe members made it clear they stood side by side with Fryberg's family: "It is our custom to come together in times of grief. The tribe holds up our people who are struggling through times of loss. We are supporting the family of Jaylen Fryberg in their time of loss, but that does not mean we condone his actions."[71] The aftermath of the Marysville Pilchuk rampage bears another striking similarity to Red Lake, which contrasts it from Sandy Hook, Columbine, and other non-indigenous rampage killings: the manner the Indian communities treated the deceased offender in death. Recalling that Peter Lanza had to deal with any potential funeral, burial, or cremation in complete secrecy, the Tulalip community treated Jaylen Fryberg's death with dignity.

The Tulalip Tribes held a funeral ritual for Jaylen Fryberg at the tribe's community center. Most significantly, more than one thousand people attended the memorial.[72] For days Fryberg's death was privately marked with traditional drumming, singing, dancing, and telling stories about his life.[73]

In the two distinct school rampage murder cases involving American Indian communities, namely Red Lake and Tulalip, the families of the rampagers were not treated as pariahs or accomplices, but as fellow victims. The tribes did not vilify the parents of the shooters for providing access to the fatal weapons. These two

Indian communities allowed the deceased killers to be treated with dignity, even in the aftermath of the bloodbaths they committed.

On February 20, 2014, Cherie Lash Rhoades, a member of the Cedarville Rancheria, a tribe of the Northern Paiute people in Alturas, California, killed four members of the tribe and injured two others during a meeting held at tribal headquarters.[74] The victims included Rhoades's brother, Rurik Davis, her niece Angel Penn, her nephew Glenn Calonicco, and tribal administrator Sheila Russo.[75] At the end of 2016, Rhoades was tried before a jury in Placer County, California.[76] The prosecutor in the case, Modoc County district attorney Jordan Funk, pursued the death penalty and the jury found Rhoades guilty of capital murder.[77] As with any capital sentence, her case is expected to be appealed.

According to the Tulare County Sheriff's Department (California), on December 10, 2012, thirty-one-year-old Hector Celaya of the Tule River Indian Reservation shot and killed four family members—his eight-year-old daughter, his mother, and two of his uncles—and wounded his two other children. The killing spree started on the reservation and ended in his automobile about twenty miles from the reservation. Celaya was killed by Tulare County sheriff's deputies.[78]

On November 22, 2014, at the Lake Traverse Indian Reservation of South Dakota, twenty-two-year-old Colter Richard Arbach went to the private residence of his girlfriend, Karissa DogEagle, where the two of them had an argument. Arbach shot and killed three of her friends and wounded her before killing himself.[79] The reservation is home to the Sisseton-Wahpeton Oyate Tribe.[80]

In recent rampage murders occurring on American Indian reservations or affecting Indian people, the victim and community responses to the incidents set the stage for examination of the social and legal responses to rampage murders occurring in non-indigenous society. The next chapter examines the more common expressions of rage, sorrow, and legal rights by victims and their families in and out of court.

The Typical Aftermath of Rampage Murder

The Outpouring of Anger at Parents and Family Members

The Impact of Advised Silence

In this chapter, I look at the community response to the parents of other non-indigenous mass shooters when the parents, themselves, were not victims. I then look at examples of community or victim-family forgiveness of parents of shooters.

Surviving parents and other immediate family members of those killed and injured by rampagers most typically focus intense anger upon their attackers. They look for answers. They want to know why their loved ones were attacked. They want to know the details of how their loved ones died. They look to make sense out of horrific incidents that make no sense. It is also common for family members of victims to focus blame on the shooter, or anyone who contributed to the criminal conduct. Law enforcement officials and criminal prosecutors sometimes bring criminal charges against the mass shooter's accomplices.[1] Prosecutors have great discretion in whether to seek charges against accomplices; the procedures for deciding when charges are brought, in general, vary from state to state and from tribe to tribe. In addition to prosecutors filing criminal charges when they can, civil litigation on behalf of surviving victims or their families is also common.

Columbine High School: Anger at and Blame of the Parents

About ten years after the tragedy at Columbine, the mother of seventeen-year-old shooter Dylan Klebold, Susan Klebold, ended her silence and wrote a moving article in *O, the Oprah Magazine*, titled "I Will Never Know Why."[2] In this article she explains her surprise and shock that her son was one of the shooters in this mass killing that killed thirteen. "None of us could accept that he was capable of doing what he did," she wrote.[3] Like many mass shootings, warning signs were missed. "He'd written a school paper about a man in a black trench coat who brutally murders nine students. But we'd never seen that paper."[4]

One author who has studied the Columbine High School murders believes that Harris and Klebold's motives have been completely misunderstood.[5] Dave Cullen, author of *Columbine*, believes Harris, in particular, was obsessed with trying to kill more people and become a bigger story than Timothy McVeigh, the Oklahoma man who killed 168 people while bombing the Alfred P. Murrah Federal Office Building in Oklahoma City. He considered Harris a terrorist whose bombs mostly failed to detonate.[6] "The audience," wrote Cullen, "for Timothy McVeigh, Eric Harris, or the Palestinian Liberation Organization—was miles away, watching on TV."[7] Speaking about Harris' objective of topping McVeigh, he wrote: "He didn't just fail to top Timothy McVeigh's record—he wasn't even recognized for trying. He was never categorized with his peer group. We lumped him in with the pathetic loners who shot people."[8]

Susan Klebold reported being "nearly insane with sorrow for the suffering her son caused."[9] At the same time she was simultaneously suffering as a parent in mourning over the loss of her son. She then reported the community response:

> But while I perceived myself to be a victim of the tragedy, I didn't have the comfort of being perceived that way by the community. I was widely viewed as a perpetrator or at least an accomplice since I was the person who raised a "monster." In one newspaper survey, 83 percent of respondents said that the parents' failure to teach Dylan and Eric proper values played a major part in the Columbine killings. If I turned on the radio, I heard angry voices condemning us for Dylan's actions. Our elected officials stated publicly that bad parenting was the cause of the massacre.[10]

The anger at and blame of the parents of shooters, as was the case with the parents of Dylan Klebold and Eric Harris, is common to other rampage shootings.

The 1997 school shootings at Heath High School in Kentucky are an excellent case study.

Wayne Steger, the father of fifteen-year-old Kayce Steger, murdered at Heath High School by Michael Carneal, said:

> We wanted . . . someone to accept the blame, the guilt, for my daughter's murder, and even today I haven't gotten that. Because [Michael] never accepted the guilt. The parents say it wasn't their fault, the shooter says, "Well I'm not accepting fault," so my daughter just went to school one day, got a hole in her head, never came home, and that's nobody's fault? That's hard to live with.[11]

Steger's comment reflects the frustrations that surviving victims, family members of victims, and their broader communities experience following mass shootings. The Heath, Kentucky, case is an excellent study that magnifies why the vertical system of justice common to non-indigenous systems of justice is a caldron for boiling anger and resentment.

Heath, Kentucky: Criminal Court Proceedings against Michael Carneal

Michael Carneal was fourteen years old when he committed the shooting at Heath High School.[12] Carneal knew his victims as fellow classmates, and some considered him a friend. The day of the shooting, he stood to the side as a group of fellow students were having a morning prayer circle in the school lobby.[13] With a handgun he stole from his friend's father, he shot eight students in the prayer circle, killing three and injuring five. Carneal was questioned by the McCracken County Sheriff's Office after the shooting and gave a confession. Without his parents or an attorney present, he told the detectives, "I guess I just got mad 'cause everybody kept making fun of me."[14] The students in the prayer circle were not, in any way, connected to anyone who made fun of Carneal.

Missy Jenkins, a friend of Carneal, was seriously injured in the rampage, left partially paralyzed and confined to a wheelchair for life. Shortly after the incident, John and Ann Carneal, Michael's parents, got permission to visit Jenkins as she was recuperating in the hospital.[15] The Carneals were clearly upset, in shock over what their son had done. It was a brief and awkward visit, but the Carneals did offer a vague apology: "It was a bit uncomfortable because there wasn't a whole lot we could say to each other," said Jenkins. "They said they were sorry for what happened, but that was the only reference [any] of us made to the shooting."[16]

Carneal was originally charged as an adult with three counts of murder, five counts of attempted murder, and one count of burglary.[17] In October 1998, Carneal pleaded "guilty but mentally ill" under Kentucky law.[18] The sentencing hearing offered very little satisfaction to the survivors or their families. It was a brief hearing presided over by Judge Jeffrey Hines. There was no trial. Carneal did not make any statement, whatsoever. He offered no apology, and did not ask for forgiveness.[19] He did not speak. Carneal's attorney, Thomas Osborn, made a brief statement on Carneal's behalf in which he claimed his client was remorseful. Carneal entered into a plea agreement with the State of Kentucky and was sentenced by Judge Hines to the maximum allowed sentence: life in prison without the possibility of parole for twenty-five years.[20]

Judge Hines allowed surviving victims or victims' family members to speak. Sebrina Steger, mother of Kayce Steger, spoke. And she directed her sad thoughts to Judge Hines:

> Kayce's murder . . . has affected every aspect of our lives, from our daily routines to our belief system. Not only have we lost our daughter, but we have lost being a normal family. We have lost the ability to be the parents we want to be to our surviving children. . . . We have a life sentence of grief. We have no hope of parole.[21]

One victim, Missy Jenkins, pushed her wheelchair past Carneal's parents and stared hard at Carneal. She insisted he confront what his gunshots had done to her body:

> I want Michael to look at me. I want to tell you that I'm paralyzed from my chest down. . . . I really feel helpless. I can't go to the bathroom like regular people. It is hard to get dressed. . . . I have to live like this every day. . . . I don't know why you did this to me and to everybody else, but I know I'm not going to forget it, because I see it every day in my mind. . . . I don't have any hard feelings towards you. . . . I can live [that] way. It's going to be hard, but I can do it.[22]

Stephen Keene, the older brother of Craig Keene, wounded by Carneal, punctuated his speech with a demand for accountability by Carneal:

Michael, I watched you gun down three girls. . . . I watched you shoot my brother and try to kill him and four other people. . . . You look at me right now! [Carneal looked up.] Thank you. . . . I don't know what was going on in your head. What would drive somebody to do this? Respond! . . . I wish I could just hide [like you]. . . . Today you will get sentenced. Today you will spend the rest of your life in jail.[23]

Advised Silence

Why did Carneal maintain silence at the sentencing hearing? He could have turned to the victims and their families and spoken, even read a carefully prepared and reviewed statement, but did not. As a criminal defense attorney, I would have advised a similarly situated criminal defendant client to be extremely cautious about making any statements, whatsoever, due to the following concerns:

1. The statement might not come out as attorney and client plan and it could become a reason for the judge to deny a plea or it could become the basis for a more severe sentence.
2. The statement might not come out as attorney and client plan and it is used against the defendant in future parole hearings.
3. The statement could be used against the defendant in future appellate hearings.
4. In the event an appeal is successful and the case is remanded for a new trial, the statement could be used against the defendant in a subsequent trial.
5. The statement could be used against the defendant or the defendant's family in future civil litigation for money damages.

Thus, once a person is represented by an attorney, a wall of silence is often constructed by attorneys seeking to protect clients. That is exactly what happened in the Heath, Kentucky, case.

Civil Litigation against Michael Carneal and His Parents

A civil suit was filed in the Circuit Court, McCracken County, Kentucky, one year after the shooting, by the families of several of the victims' families.[24] The plaintiffs alleged that Michael Carneal's parents "knew or should have known that Michael was a troubled child with violent tendencies," and that they nevertheless "kept several weapons in their home, including pistols and rifles . . . [and] failed to properly secure the weapons in the house."[25] The complaint further alleged that Carneal's parents "negligently and recklessly failed to prevent the shootings."[26] In an amendment to the original complaint, plaintiffs added that the parents "owed a duty to exercise ordinary care to prevent their son [Michael] from harming others . . . [and the parents] breached this duty of ordinary care."[27]

In the complaint the plaintiffs further alleged that "as the natural parents of Michael Carneal, [the parents] had a special power of control over his conduct," giving rise to the duty to "prevent their son from intentionally injuring [others] or to prevent [their son] from creating an unreasonable risk of harm to [others]."[28] Carneal's parents, according to the complaint, "permitted their irresponsible son to run at large."[29] Finally, because his parents believed "their son to be mentally ill, and thus not responsible for his actions," the plaintiffs alleged that Michael Carneal became "the conduit" of his parents under the law, and thus, his parents should have been held vicariously liable for their son's actions.[30] The plaintiffs sought not only compensatory but also punitive damages against both parents of the shooter.[31]

At this stage of the proceedings, before the criminal and civil cases were adjudicated, Michael Carneal and his parents had every incentive to say as little as possible. Their cautious strategy to limit what they said, and uphold an out-of-court silence, had an impact on the civil suit.[32] The trial court's Special Judge William L. Shadoan granted the defendant's motion for summary judgment, finding no breach of duty on the part of the parents. In April 2002, the Kentucky Court of Appeals issued an opinion affirming the summary judgment ruling in favor of Michael Carneal's parents, disposing them of the parental liability claim.[33] The court said, "Appellants have failed to present any evidence which shows that the Carneals knew or should have known that they needed to exercise the control over their son necessary to prevent him from shooting his classmates."[34]

Civil suits like the negligence suit filed against Michael Carneal's parents after the Heath High School shooting are not uncommon.[35] Victims have also filed suits seeking damages from a wide variety of other potential tortfeasors, like the manufacturers of the guns the shooters used or pharmaceuticals the shooters had taken.[36] Thus, victims look for accountability and seek answers. They try to make sense out of something that cannot be made sensible. As a result they take actions into their own hands. Ironically, in doing so, they actually contribute to the conditions that block their access to people they desperately seek answers, explanations, and justice from.

The frustration felt by victims of rampage shootings when they cannot get answers was summarized by Missy Jenkins: "What Michael did to us that day still doesn't make sense. No matter how many different answers I get from court depositions, psychological evaluations, people who knew him, or Michael himself, I don't think I'll ever fully understand it."[37]

Thus the walls of silence that are built by the Western system of vertical criminal and civil justice leaves mass shooting victims demanding accountability with no ability to get it. It leaves the shooters and the parents of the shooters in a horrible morass of guilt and shame. It provides for no meaningful dialogue between culpable parties and those mourning horrible grief.

Victims Cry Out for Closure: A Case Study

The frustrations of criminal case participants in Anglo-European courts are not limited to mass murder cases. I have focused on those cases because they present broader community and societal impact. The same frustrations are played out in courtrooms every day wherever silence of participants is advisable and protected.

I was hired as an expert witness to review a criminal trial and to testify in a 2014 habeas corpus trial in Connecticut. That case, *State of Connecticut v. Chadwick St. Louis*, provides one glimpse into the frustrations present in the Anglo-European system of criminal justice.[38]

In May of 2009 in Hartford, Connecticut, Chadwick St. Louis was tried and convicted of the 2006 murder of twenty-four-year-old Christopher Petrozza. Petrozza's family considered St. Louis a family friend and a very close friend of Petrozza. A three-judge panel concluded that St. Louis murdered Petrozza and then buried his body in St. Louis's backyard. The panel also concluded that St. Louis engaged in a lengthy pattern of deception to hide Petrozza's disappearance and St. Louis's role in the crime.

Typically, in Connecticut, witnesses are not allowed to attend a trial if they are scheduled to testify; they are sequestered.[39] The intention of an order to sequester witnesses is to prevent witnesses from shaping their testimony to corroborate falsely with the testimony of others.[40] An exception is often made for members of the family of the defendant or the victim's immediate family, as was done in this case. Without this exception, the families of the participants become even more alienated from the proceedings.

St. Louis did not testify during any portion of his original trial or the sentencing hearing. This was a conscious decision of the defendant after consultation with his attorney. His attorney, Dennis McMahon, took the position at trial that Petrozza's death was the result of an accident. If St. Louis testified at his trial or spoke at his sentencing hearing, his words could have been used by the state of Connecticut in any of several post-conviction proceedings that took place or at a retrial had St. Louis prevailed in an appeal. In fact, St. Louis's case had numerous post-conviction proceedings: two appeals, one petition for sentence review, and a petition for habeas corpus.[41]

Family members of Petrozza were understandably despondent by Petrozza's disappearance and St. Louis's role in his death. Several of them spoke at the sentencing hearing. There they all sat, in one room together, the families of the victim and murderer. One theme was repeated. Petrozza's family wanted to know what exactly happened to their son and brother. They wanted to know what his last words were. They never got to say goodbye.

There was no testimony as to exactly how Petrozza died. No eye witness testified. Even the State Medical Examiner, Ira Kanfer, who testified, was vague about how Petrozza might have died.[42] Petrozza's body lay in a hole for many months before it was ultimately discovered and examined. The vertical justice system left a deep and emotional void.

Petrozza's mother, Janet Allegra, said to the judges, "Chad saw Christopher's body lying dead. He knows what Christopher's last words were."[43] Petrozza's sister, Heather Petrozza, begged for a face-to-face meeting with St. Louis. She begged for answers:

> And once this is all over and Chad is sentence[d] I would pray to God that even if it takes 20 years that he will sit down and look me in the face and tell me what happened. Just me and him. Once it's all over, no judges, nothing. I need to know. I don't care how awful it is; I need to know. I need to know if my brother laid there crying, looking up at Chad asking why, what [was] the look on his face; "Why would you do this to me, I loved you." I need to know if he wanted to say goodbye to us. Did my brother look at Chad and say "please say goodbye to my family"?[44]

Heather Petrozza next addressed St. Louis: "I need to know what happened, Chad.

I need to sit down and talk and I know that I'm the one person that you will talk to. Please, when this is all over, no more lies."[45] Petrozza's stepfather, Arthur Allegra, also spoke to St. Louis, echoing Heather's plea for a meeting and for answers: "We trusted you, and like Heather said, you need to come and fess up. You need to tell somebody."[46]

Before he sentenced St. Louis to fifty years in prison, Judge Thomas P. Miano, one of the three judges who presided over the case, addressed Petrozza's family, their demand for answers, and their plea for an explanation from St. Louis. Miano confessed his lack of background in psychology:

> In my opinion and I'm not one that's sophisticated in things of the mind or sociology or psychology or psychiatry, but in my opinion, if you truly love someone really truly there will never be closure and it troubles me as a lay person, not being sophisticated in this area, when I hear the family saying we want to hear how it ended, how it happened. Well, I can't fully appreciate your situation. Certainly my heart goes out to the family for their loss but I can't fully appreciate it, because you may never know, and I think you've got to find other ways to heal, as the Judge has indicated, and I'm certain that's what Christopher would have wanted. But to hinge your hopes on what the Defendant may say I think is a false sense of hope, in my lay opinion, as a lay person not sophisticated in this area.[47]

On July 7, 2014, St. Louis finally spoke. He testified at the habeas corpus hearing where his primary claim was the ineffectiveness of McMahon, his trial counsel. He claimed Petrozza died in a construction accident involving excavating equipment. The habeas trial court did not find his testimony credible. Eight years after the murder and five years after the first trial, the Petrozza family at least got to hear St. Louis's version of how their son and brother died. They were present in the courtroom. They never got the face-to-face dialogue they craved.

The failure of the Anglo-European criminal justice model to provide face-to-face interaction in murder cases has been exposed in this chapter, detailing cases where victims or their families have expressed a desire for interaction. The walls of separation erected between offenders and victims, along with the impact of what I call "advised silence," leaves a trail of profound individual and collective dissatisfaction. In the next chapter, I examine the history of restorative justice in certain indigenous cultures, which includes examples of families of offenders and their victims talking things out.

Restorative Justice in Indigenous Cultures

Restoring Balance and Harmony

Where there is community dissatisfaction with the handling of criminal justice, there is often a parallel lack of community involvement. Restorative justice differs from traditional concepts of criminal justice in that the conflict is between an individual and either another individual, a group of individuals, or the community as a whole, rather than between an individual and the state.[1]

The talking-things-out approach after an offense among the extended families of both the offender and the victim, which exists in many indigenous cultures, provides that escape valve for serious emotional outpouring of emotion. It allows victims to demand answers, to sit face to face with offenders and ask "why." The emotional escape valve is severely lacking in Anglo-European adversarial systems of justice. In the mass murders and rampage killings discussed in this book, talking things out would accomplish an important social function.

Herein lies the juxtaposition between Anglo-European vertical systems, and indigenous horizontal systems.[2] The history of indigenous justice systems goes back many centuries, and there are many examples throughout the world.

The Anglo-European transition from a system of kin-based dispute resolution gave way to the litigation-and-court system in which feudal lords retained part of the property forfeited by the offender.[3] In England a loose system of feudal lords and property forfeiture was centralized and then consolidated during the century following the Norman Invasion of 1066, with the development of state/crown law, which depended on the collection of revenue by the judge, specifically for the king. This transformation completed the transference of focus from the victim to the state. The decline of compensation to the victim was the second change.[4]

The modern system of justice is also sometimes referred to as the "retributive model" of justice.[5] However, our English language criminal justice vocabulary has many origins in restorative justice concepts. The Greek word *pune* referred to an exchange of money for a harm caused.[6] The English word "guilt" likely derives from the Anglo-Saxon *geldan*, which, like the German word *geld*, refers to payment.[7]

There is debate in the academic community whether the efforts by criminologists and criminal justice practitioners to document international traditions of restorative justice is entirely accurate.[8] The academic debate surrounding the roots of restorative justice notwithstanding, there is a rich history of indigenous individualized systems of traditional justice throughout the world. Whereas restorative practices were the predominant characteristic of traditional dispute resolution methodologies, punitive practices, no doubt, also existed.[9] Detailed here is an overview of criminal dispute resolution among indigenous peoples of North America, with a more precise focus on two peoples, the Navajo and the Cheyenne.

There are great differences in historical approaches to justice among indigenous peoples in the United States. The one consistent concept among indigenous peoples in precontact America is the focus on reparations and making victims or their families "whole" after some injury.[10] In this period, it appears that even killings were considered repairable wrongs.[11] A second fundamental principle common to many American Indian people is the spiritual basis of much traditional indigenous law.[12] A distinctive worldview influences many tribal practices, ideals, and law.[13]

One comprehensive explanation of North American sacred ways explains a worldview shared by many:

> One of the important concepts Native American tribal people share with respect to the sacred is that all things in the universe are dependent on each other. This concept is first introduced to a child through the stories and songs of the origin histories. Behind the ceremonials and rituals each tribe carries out throughout the

year is the notion of balance and imbalance. Disease is seen as part of the total environment which would include the individual, the community, the natural world of ancestors and spirits.[14]

In this explanation, the concept of "balance" has two important elements. First, it is grounded in a sacred order that is connected to a great spirit or some other supernatural force, which is associated with sacred ritual. Second, it is expansive, with distinct social dimensions, and includes proper familial relationships within clans and with other familial relationships, the natural world, and spirits.[15]

The methods of making people whole among American Indian cultures has varied. For example, the Ojibwe, a major component group of the Anishinaabe-speaking peoples in North America, focused on cleansing spirits of both the victim and the offender as a method of repairing injuries done to both and of aiding their futures as community members.[16] This contrasts with a focus on blame and punishment.

The Inuit, a North American indigenous people occupying what are now the Arctic regions of Alaska, Canada, and Greenland, went to great length to avoid even the perception of offender punishment. They held community meetings that focused on the event and possible solutions to hypothetical future events.[17]

The Iroquois were a confederation of several tribes of indigenous people, inhabiting what is now the Northeastern United States and parts of Canada. Among the Iroquois, a killer's family would meet with the killer to attempt to persuade him or her to confess guilt. If the killer did confess, the family of the killer would send a strip of white wampum, which are beads made from clams, to the victim's family or clan to signal their desire to make reparations.[18] The wampum might be accepted and the death pardoned. If the wampum was refused, the refusal meant that the victim's family would retaliate and claim a killing within the killer's family or clan.[19] Sometimes the killer's family reacted with a decision to kill the offender themselves, which would protect the clan from revenge.[20]

The Iroquois employed mourning rituals after a crisis. These mourning rituals were common among American Indian Woodlands tribes.[21] The Iroquois ceremony was called the Condolence Council and was wholly consistent with the American Indian belief that relationships of close connection were sustained by shared suffering and solidarity in times of crisis.[22] Aspects of the Iroquois mourning ritual included the smoking of a sacred pipe and sharing the same bowl to eat together. The ritual included telling stories spoken by the wampum that rekindled the fire to bind the mourners close together and, significantly, of wiping away any bad blood between the two sides.[23]

The Karuk, an indigenous people inhabiting what is now the state of California, utilized a system of compensation for all crimes, including death.[24] In this system, crimes could be forgiven as long as sufficient compensation was given. Compensation was not always in the form of remuneration. Sometimes it involved caring for the victims' family, or "waiting on" an injured victim.[25]

Compensation and the Crow Dog Case

The Crow Dog murder case of 1881 is illustrative of how some American Indian tribes resolved murder cases with compensation from the offender to the family of the victim.[26] Both Crow Dog (birth name: Kan-gi-shun-ca) and Spotted Tail (birth name: Sinte Gleska) were members of the Brule Sioux band of the Sioux Nation of Indians—Spotted Tail was recognized by the Sioux as a great chief.[27]

Crow Dog, a warrior, killed Spotted Tail in what appears to have been an attempt to usurp the chief's power.[28] The Sioux Nation dealt with the murder in the traditional Sioux method of dispute resolution. Peacemakers were sent to meet with both families. The matter was settled tribally with six hundred dollars in cash, eight horses, and one blanket given to Spotted Tail's family by Crow Dog.[29] What made the case famous was that Chief Spotted Tail was well known in Washington, DC, as a leader. His reputation led to an uproar outside of Indian country after his murder that there had been no Anglo-style prosecution or penalty. A federal prosecution of Crow Dog resulted, but was unsuccessful.[30] Crow Dog's conviction was overturned by the U.S. Supreme Court on jurisdictional grounds.[31]

In addition to monetary compensation, another fairly common condition imposed by American Indian tribes in murder and other serious cases was banishment.[32] Banishment removed and ostracized the offender from the community, a serious consequence, as food and safety were collaborative community efforts. Scholars have referred to banishment in precolonial Africa as a "social death."[33] In one North American case where there was an unintentional killing, the Cherokee allowed the offender to flee to a "sacred city of refuge" where they would be safe from possible revenge.[34]

Navajo

The Navajo (or Diné) are an indigenous people who live in what is now the southwest of the United States. Traditional Navajo concepts of justice are rooted with healing as the goal. Central to obtaining healing is the Navajo concept of *hózhó*. This concept is not easily translated, but it loosely means harmony and balance.[35] "Traditional Navajos understand *Diné bi beenahaz'áanii* as values, norms, customs and traditions that are transmitted orally across generations and which produce and maintain right relations, right relationships, and desirable outcomes in Navajo society."[36]

Proper social relationships are critical to achieving *hózhó*. The Navajo have a complex system of kinship and clans (*k'ei*), and requirements of kinship solidarity, or *k'e*. According to Navajo jurist and scholar, Raymond Austin, kinship is of the utmost importance to the Navajo, as clan relatives provide the essentials a Navajo needs for physical, mental, emotional, and spiritual well-being.[37] *K'e* includes taking personal responsibility for achieving harmony with valuable members of one's family and clan, with whom each person is firmly linked. The purpose of the Navajo concept of justice is to bring finality to the issue at hand, correct the imbalances, and bring all parties back to *hózhó*.[38] By talking things out with respect under the principles of *k'e*, the Navajo bring those in conflict into *hózhó*.[39]

Modern Navajo peacemaking efforts derive from traditional principles of justice and are premised upon participation by all those affected, including victims. According to Philmer Bluehouse and James W. Zion, "The Navajo horizontal (peace planning) system of justice uses Navajo norms, values, moral principles, and emotions as law. *K'e* and *k'ei* are only two of these precepts. There are many others that apply to healing situations and are expressed in Navajo creation and journey scripture, songs, ceremonies, and prayers."[40]

One ceremony, or ritual, in particular, is important to peacemaking: the Blessingway Ceremony. Navajos regard the Blessingway Ceremony as an important backbone of their beliefs.[41] Among other uses, Navajo employ this ritual to "avert misfortune, to invoke positive blessings that man needs for a long and happy life."[42] It is a ritual that can last two days.

This comprehensive peacemaking process is used to reach a consensus among all participants, which is critical to resolution of the dispute, concern, or issue. With full voluntary participation (*t'áá altso athil ka'iijée'go*) and consensus, a resolution is reached with all participants giving their sacred word (*hazaad jidísingo*) that they will abide by the decision. The resolution (guided by the concept of *Diné bi beenahaz'áanii*), in turn, is the basis for restoring harmony (*bee hózhǫ́náhodoodleeł*). *Hózhǫ́* is established if all who participated in the peacemaking process are committed to the agreement and consider it as the final agreement from which the parties can proceed to live in harmony again. Finality is established when all participants agree that all of the concerns or issues have been comprehensively resolved in the agreement (*ná bináheezláago bee t'áá łahjį́ ałgha' deet'ą́*).[43] The participation of the community in resolving disputes between parties is a deep-seated part of Navajo collective identity and is central to the Navajo way of government.[44]

Traditional Navajo Method of Resolving Homicides and Other Violent Offenses

As an offense, homicide was uncommon among Navajo in the nineteenth and early twentieth centuries.[45] Before 1810 the predominant cause of homicide was interclan or family feuds, domestic matters, or personal insult. Following the introduction of liquor in 1810, intoxication became the predominant cause of homicide.[46] Traditionally, murders were resolved among Navajo people where the family of the victim made a demand of retribution, first in the form of payment of goods, which initially included shells, gems, or hides, and later came to involve animals, or live stock.[47] Four horses were the price for the murder of a man, for example. If the demanded payment was not made, the immediate family of the offender was held responsible. If payment was still withheld, the death penalty was applied to the offender.[48]

An "accidental" death was still considered a homicide to the Navajo and relatives of the deceased sought payment. If payment was refused, "blood revenge" was sought.[49] For lesser injuries the traditional custom of "A Clothes," was employed, where the family of an injured Navajo person would forfeit clothing; the amount of clothing corresponded to the depth of the wound.[50] Retribution in the form of compensation was significant to the Navajo as wealth was an important aspect throughout traditional Navajo culture.[51]

Cheyenne

The Cheyenne were an indigenous people living in the Midwestern American Plains and were part of the Algonquin group of tribes. After 1833 they were divided into a northern division, which included southeastern Montana and eastern Wyoming, and a southern division, which included western Oklahoma and eastern Colorado. Cheyenne existence was a nomadic, semipastoral, and hunting-based life.[52] The Cheyenne were governed by an organization that consisted of two orders: the tribal chiefs comprising of a council of forty-four, and military (soldier) societies.[53] Both groups participated in the process of deciding how homicide cases were resolved.[54]

Homicide cases that occurred where the offender was from an enemy tribe were handled differently than when the offenders were also Cheyenne. Regarded as an unusual occurrence, there is a reported case in the nineteenth century where the Cheyenne community sought revenge for the murder of two Cheyenne brothers by members of the enemy Crow tribe. In this case, which was the murder of the sons of Red Robe, many Cheyenne people charged into the Crow camp, killing many Crows.[55] In some ways the Red Robe case more resembles intertribal warfare than it does individual criminal dispute resolution.

Karl N. Llewellyn and E. Adamson Hoebel report that there were sixteen homicides in the Cheyenne community from 1835 to 1879.[56] When one Cheyenne murdered another, it was viewed as a sin that "bloodied the Sacred Arrows," and endangered the entire tribe. After committing a murder, the Cheyenne believed that the offender began an internal disintegration that had a corresponding odor. The tribe could purify itself by eliminating the taint through banishment of the murderer.[57] Thus, while banishment had a punitive affect, the purpose for the Cheyenne was not to punish but to cure a wound suffered by the community.

After a murder the tribal chiefs would convene a conference. The military society performed an investigative function. A decree of banishment followed, though the decree was not permanent. It was an indeterminate sentence where commutation of the sentence would occur on several alternative grounds. Commutation of a murder sentence required consent by the council, the military agency, and the father of the victim. An offering of tobacco as an expression of contrition was also common among the Cheyenne.[58]

The case of the murder of Cheyenne Chief Eagle by Cries Yia Eya is a good example of how an indeterminate murder sentence was eventually commuted. Sometime between 1860 and 1890, Cries Yia Eya killed Chief Eagle in what is referred to as a "whiskey brawl."[59] The chiefs banished Cries Yia Eya. One day Cries Yia Eya returned to the exterior of the Cheyenne camp with bundles of tobacco, sending word that he was "begging to come home."[60] The tobacco was intended for distribution among the tribe.

After a debate among the various soldier societies, one soldier announced that he believed the "stink" associated with a murderer had "blown from [Cries Yia Eya]."[61] The soldiers then attempted to persuade the father of Chief Eagle to allow Cries Yia Eya to return and to accept the tobacco. Chief Eagle's father agreed, so long as Cries Yia Eya vowed to conduct himself appropriately in the future. Cries Yia Eya was allowed to return.

Even after being allowed to return to the community, though, murderers still suffered a level of ostracism. It is reported, at least in one case, that the murderer could never again touch their lips to the tobacco pipe of another man nor eat from another man's bowls.[62] Regarding banishment, Pawnee, a Southern Cheyenne chief who had behaved badly as a young man, said: "You may run away, but your people will always remember."[63]

The history of the resolution of murders among indigenous peoples reveals many common themes. Community participation by elders or community leaders is one commonality, and a dialogue between the families of offenders and the families of victims is another. Overall, the restoration of social harmony was a common goal; taking the offense out of the offender is also a repeated commonality. Dispute resolution in murder cases had a spiritual component to them. Although there are examples among indigenous peoples in which murderers were punished, even by death, compensation for the death was common. Still, many communities demonstrated peace among combatants with the sharing of a meal, or eating together from the same bowl of food. Some level of community ostracism of the offender is another commonality.

The history of serious criminal case dispute resolution among two indigenous cultures in North America are chronicled in this chapter, and a wide range of restorative practices are highlighted. An important cross-cultural component was a requirement of forgiveness, which, to cite one example, was the prerequisite for allowing a banished murderer to return to the community. A deep understanding of forgiveness and its place in the discourse of the aftermath of murder is the subject of chapter 6.

Forgiveness

Restoring Social Bonds

The importance of forgiveness to healing and reconciliation cannot be overstated. In fact, Archbishop Desmond Tutu says that "without forgiveness there is no future."[1]

Forgiveness is complex the product of a number of contributing factors, among them depression, commitment to apology, and empathy.[2] It is so complex and weighty that the philosopher Friedrich Nietzsche viewed it with a healthy measure of skepticism. He viewed forgiveness as offered reluctantly as a result of an unequal power dynamic with typically limited choice as to whether to offer it.[3] Forgiveness is effective, though. It heals. There is evidence that forgiveness interventions increase the level of potential forgiveness following an offense, and that those interventions "increase hope and psychological well-being, and decrease depression, anxiety, and anger."[4]

Forgiveness: What Exactly Is It?

Researchers have come to a consensus that forgiveness can include: (1) a reduction in "vengeful and angry thoughts, feelings, and motives," which may coincide with

(2) an increase in "positive thoughts, feelings, and motives toward the offending person."[5] In other words, forgiveness refers to a voluntary behavioral change toward a perceived transgressor, and includes the reduction of negative thoughts, emotions, and motivations toward the transgressor, which might cause eventual changed behaviors.[6]

Forgiveness is, therefore, understood largely as an intrapersonal experience that does not necessarily include reconciliation with the offending person even though reconciliation might accompany it. There is further consensus among researchers that forgiveness does not mean condoning, forgetting, or excusing the wrongdoing and that it is not just the opposite or absence of vengefulness and bitterness.[7] School shooting survivor Missy Jenkins said, "Forgiving someone can lift an enormous burden of our shoulders and allow us to concentrate on our recovery."[8]

Are horrific rampages such as the school shootings at Columbine High School, Virginia Tech, Sandy Hook Elementary School, and Red Lake High School too serious to introduce restorative justice themes? The Dalai Lama and other contemporary Buddhists "teach the West that the more evil the crime, the greater the opportunity for grace to inspire a transformative will to resist tyranny with compassion."[9] The Dalai Lama said: "Learning to forgive is much more useful than picking up a stone and throwing it at the object of one's anger, the more so when the provocation is extreme. For it is under the greatest adversity that there exists the greatest potential for doing good, both for oneself and for others."[10]

It is logical that the more serious the event, the more negative the overall impression of the offender, including rampage murders.[11] As a result, there has not been much academic attention given to this negative correlation. The negative view of the offender becomes associated with the negative event and, therefore, may produce a conclusion that the offender is undeserving of forgiveness.[12] Victims, then, might avoid interaction with or even contemplate revenge against the offender who commits a serious offense, the victim desiring not to be victimized again in the future.[13]

Religion and Forgiveness

Where Does Our Understanding of Forgiveness Come From?

The concept of forgiveness has roots in the history of religious belief. Forgiveness and justice are central tenets of many of the world's religions.[14] In fact, the three major monotheistic religions—Judaism, Islam, and Christianity—promote forgiveness and justice not only as aspirations of religious adherents, but also as qualities of God.[15]

Jewish religious belief was the basis for Jewish law. Jewish belief and Jewish law influenced Christian philosophy. Christianity inherited from Judaism the belief in a God who is thought of as a loving father and a righteous judge, a paradoxical God, combining both mercy and justice.[16] Hebrew, Christian, and Islamic texts often implore adherents to practice forgiveness.[17]

In his legal treatise, *Mishneh Torah*, Jewish scholar and Talmudist Rabbi Moshe ben Nachman (1194–1270), also referred to as Nachmanides, wrote that where there are sins between man and man, those sins will never be forgiven until the offending person "gives his colleague what he owes him and appeases him."[18] Apology, restitution, and forgiveness are essential tenets of the Jewish faith. The holiest day of the year for Jews is Yom Kippur, which translates as "the Day of Atonement."

The threat of eternal punishment and the corresponding emphasis on repentance and forgiveness is more pronounced in the Christian New Testament than it is in the Hebrew Bible.[19] Christian philosophy and belief was a pronounced influence over the common law.[20] Christian philosopher Saint Anselm (1033–1109) developed a tenet called the Doctrine of Atonement.[21] Anselm's theory emphasized the humanity of the Son of God, who suffered death as an appeasement of sin. This allowed God to forgive, and at the same time gave man the ability to accept forgiveness and then be redeemed.[22]

In Christian belief, forgiveness is an important element of justice, as is punishment. Both are required, neither one alone suffices. God alone cannot forgive man's sins: "This would leave the disturbance of the order of the universe, caused by sin, uncorrected, and that uncorrected disorder would constitute a deficiency in justice." "Mercy," said Anselm," is the daughter of justice; it is derived from justice and cannot work against justice."[23]

For many people the term "spiritual" more closely defines their belief system than "religious." "Spirituality" is defined as a person's search for a sense of closeness or connection with the sacred.[24] "Sacred" is what a person believes to be set apart from the ordinary, and therefore deserving of veneration.[25] Most people in the United States experience the sacred as God or some divine being within the context of a specific religious tradition.[26] Others, like many indigenous peoples, experience a connection or closeness to nature, humanity, or the universe.

When Religious People Are Victims of Rampage Murder

Alissa and Robbie Parker's willingness to meet with the father of the young man who committed the horrific murder of their six-year-old daughter, Emilie, and their willingness to forgive were, no doubt, influenced by their backgrounds as active members of the Church of Jesus Christ of Latter-day Saints.[27]

The aftermath of the school shooting at Heath High School in West Paducah, Kentucky, was very much influenced by Christian ideology and the centrality of forgiveness in the belief system of a religious community. The shooting took place, after all, at a prayer circle at a public high school. The day after the shooting, school children hung a sign at the school that said, "We forgive you because God forgave us."[28] While still in the emergency room recovering from critical injuries, Missy Jenkins forgave the shooter, fourteen-year-old Michael Carneal, which surprised many people. She credited her church baptism two years earlier:

> Maybe it stemmed from my baptism less than two years earlier in the eighth grade. That momentous night in front of that congregation had strengthened my faith to the point where as a teenager, my relationship with God was as strong as it ever had been. Faith, hope, love, understanding, charity: I was fortunate, at such a young age, that they were all at the forefront of my life. And so was forgiveness.[29]

Like Alissa and Robbie Parkers in Newtown, who publicly forgave the killer of their daughter, Emilie, and then had a face-to-face meeting with her killer's father, Missy Jenkins, too, met face to face with Michael Carneal, the boy who paralyzed her.

The aftermath of a rampage affecting a highly religious Amish community in Pennsylvania closely resembled the community responses exhibited in the two American Indian cultures of the Red Lake Chippewa and the Tulalip Indian Tribes.

The Amish School Shooting, Nickel Mines, Pennsylvania

On October 2, 2006, Charles Carl Roberts barricaded himself in a one-room Amish school house in Nickel Mines, Pennsylvania. Roberts killed six girls ages seven to thirteen before killing himself.[30] Viewing Roberts's family as victims, too, Amish parents immediately sent messages of forgiveness to them.[31] The Amish are deeply devout people. Their roots date back to the Anabaptist movement of the Protestant Reformation in sixteenth-century Europe.

Anabaptist martyrs emphasized completely turning over one's life to God. The Amish say the martyr testimony evolves from the example of Jesus, the foundation of their faith. They do not ponder if forgiveness is effective; rather, they apply it in the way they view Jesus would have responded to his adversaries, or enemies.[32]

Although Roberts had just committed an unspeakable atrocity—the murder of six innocent school girls—Roberts's family and friends had no trouble arranging a funeral service at a local funeral home. They also had no trouble arranging a burial for him, not in secrecy or the darkness of night, but in the Georgetown, Pennsylvania, United Methodist Church Cemetery a few hundred yards from his home.[33] While Roberts's crime bears a resemblance to Adam Lanza's in Newtown, the aftermath is analogous to those in the two American Indian communities studied in this book, the Red Lake Chippewa and the Tulalip Indian Tribes.

The Emanuel AME Church Shooting, Charleston, South Carolina

The case of rampage shooter Dylann Roof is another case where there was an immediate pronouncement of public forgiveness, which made his initial bond hearing unorthodox and extraordinary. Roof was arrested for the June 17, 2015, murder of nine African American adults at a Charleston, South Carolina, church.[34] In most state criminal courts, preliminary bond hearings are short, succinct matters. Prosecuting attorneys and defense lawyers make pitches to judges about whether bail and conditions of release ought to be set while a criminal case slogs through the courts. This, however, was no ordinary bail hearing.

Television cameras were rolling and the world was watching. In attendance were family members of many of the victims of the outrageous slaying. Several family members decided to speak, a right granted to victims and their family members in the wake of the laws enacted during the victim's rights movement of the 1980s and 1990s.[35] When they spoke, they spoke to Roof, who was participating in the hearing from jail via an interactive video link.

Nadine Collier was one of the family members who spoke. Roof was accused of shooting and killing Collier's seventy-year-old mother, Ethel Lance.[36] Her voice trembling with emotion, Collier said to Roof: "You took something very precious away from me. I will never talk to her again. I will never be able to hold her again. But I forgive you. And have mercy on your soul."[37]

Many other family members repeated the emotional pleas and the sentiments of forgiveness. That they could communicate kindness and keep anger to a minimum was startling for many observers.[38] Had the same comments been made one year later, they would have had much less of an impact. The public's attention span is short. That these expressions of forgiveness came with immediacy, while the world was watching, created a lasting impression for many.[39]

What made the expressions of forgiveness so unusual was not only that they were made, or how quickly after the shooting they were made, but also that they were made in an American criminal courtroom. Criminal court hearings are not the logical site for forgiveness from victims, or of interaction between offenders and their families.

Something else happened at the bond hearing that was unorthodox: the judge made a speech. With the world watching, Magistrate James B. Gosnell Jr. recognized that in American rampages, there are many victims. While it was likely the wrong time and place for the observation, he made note that even Roof's family could be considered victims of Roof's murderous spree.[40] Their lives, too, would be inextricably linked to Roof's atrocity. Some people would outright blame them, as they did the mother of Connecticut rampager, Adam Lanza.

In July 2015, Roof was indicted by a federal grand jury on thirty-three counts of federal hate crimes, weapons charges, and obstructing the practice of religion. He was convicted and, in January 2017, sentenced to death. Roof was also prosecuted by the State of South Carolina. He pleaded guilty there and was sentenced to nine consecutive life sentences.[41]

Theoretical Models of Forgiveness

Does forgiveness have a theoretical framework? Direct communication allows for dialogue, for negotiation. It allows for community involvement in the disposition of a case. It makes possible understanding, confession, reconciliation, and forgiveness.[42] Sociologist Thomas J. Scheff calls this process "symbolic reparation."[43] Symbolic reparation accompanies "material reparation," which refers to the restitution, compensation, community service paid to the victim, their family, or even the greater community.[44]

Scheff has a formula for when symbolic reparation can occur. According to Scheff, an offender must clearly express genuine shame and remorse for their actions. This expression may take the form of an apology, and research supports the close connection between forgiveness and apology.[45] The expression of shame and remorse may be followed by the victim or their family beginning the first steps to forgive the offender. Scheff calls this process the "core sequence." The crime, according to Scheff, severed a social bond between the offender and both the victim and the community.[46] The core sequence restores this bond. The offender's acceptance of responsibility paves the way for their reacceptance into the community, which makes recidivism less likely, according to Scheff.

For shame and remorse to be effective tools that contribute to healing and be accepted by surviving victims or, in restorative justice settings, by the community, it is important that these expressions be genuine. Determining when they are genuine requires skill and training, even for professionals, and might require observation over a period of time.

The Importance of Apology

As stated above, the outward expression of remorse and shame are important components to obtaining forgiveness. The apology is also an important component of this process. An apology is a validation of another person's feelings, intuition, and perception. It is one of the most effective methods for healing humiliation and generating forgiveness.[47]

As one law professor said, we live in the "age of apology," and another said that "'apology fever' is everywhere."[48] Yet, apology has often been empirically associated with forgiveness. Apology, when experienced together with restitution, has been found to be related to increased forgiveness.[49]

Obtaining closure for victims of violence and their families is a popular modern subject. The subject is frequently cited in the United States as an objective in death penalty cases.[50] There is support in research that giving crime victims input in criminal sentencing yields satisfaction. Whether victim input helps reduce their long-term trauma, however, remains to be determined.[51]

A number of theoretical models for forgiveness have been developed.[52] Research groups headed by R. D. Enright (*Forgiveness Is a Choice: A Step-by-Step Process for Resolving Anger and Restoring Hope*) and E. L. Worthington Jr. (*Five Steps to Forgiveness; The Art and Science of Forgiving*) have set forth a framework for accomplishing it.[53] Unlike the work of Thomas J. Scheff, discussed above, intrapersonal versus interpersonal models are the focus of their research.

The Importance of Face-to Face, Interpersonal Reconciliation: A Change of Heart

Some psychologists and academic scholars generally believe forgiveness to be an internal, intrapersonal process that may or may not lead to reconciliation.[54] Research reveals, though, that when surveyed, there is a variance in belief among individuals as to whether positive, interpersonal interaction with the offender is also required for complete forgiveness.[55] Further research is needed to assess the benefits of interpersonal, face-to-face interactions in reducing negative effects of heinous criminal victimization and simultaneously producing positive outcomes.

The case of Nancy Langert and her sister Jeanne Bishop is another powerful (although admittedly anecdotal) example of the importance of breaking down the wall of separation between murderers and victims and their families, and the healing potential of face-to face meetings.[56]

Having broken into their home in suburban Winnetka, Illinois in 1990, David Biro sat and waited for a young married couple to return from a family dinner. With a stolen .357 Magnum, Biro killed the young and athletic Richard Langert, execution style. He then turned his gun on Langert's twenty-five-year-old pregnant wife, Nancy, killing her. Nancy's family took a hard line on the prosecution of Biro.

Nancy Langert's sister, Jeanne Bishop, lived with decades of pain and sorrow, and hatred for Biro. After twenty years, Bishop, a practicing Christian, decided to go to the Pontiac Prison to visit her sister's killer.[57] Throughout his trial and for more than twenty years, Biro had maintained his innocence, denying the family of his victims the ability to hear his words of apology. In 2013, in the visitor room of the prison, Jeanne Bishop and David Biro met. At the meeting, Biro, for the first time, confessed his murder of Nancy and Richard Langert.[58] He told Bishop the details of her sister's violent death. Before the meeting the details of Nancy's death was a matter of mere speculation. Biro filled in the blanks. He explained himself, not making excuses, but offering the explanation of what motivated him as an adolescent to kill.

Was Biro motivated to confess by a desire to someday obtain release on parole? Perhaps, or perhaps not. Either way, Bishop experienced a sense of closure and satisfaction that only her face-to-face, interpersonal connection could produce.

Face-to-Face Healing Takes Place in Rampage Murder Cases

School Shooter Michael Carneal Meets with a Survivor

The importance of discourse between rampage shooters (or their families) and their victims (or their families) is illustrated in the case of the Heath High School shooting in West Paducah, Kentucky. The Heath shooting is an excellent case study, since it is one of the rare cases where a shooter did not die in the incident. With Michael Carneal alive, this case is remarkable because a survivor from the shooting had a prison meeting with Carneal.

On July 21, 2007, ten years after the shooting, Michael Carneal, then twenty-four years old, met with Missy Jenkins. The meeting occurred in a room in the juvenile prison where Carneal was serving his sentence, the LaGrange Reformatory. Before the shooting, Carneal and Jenkins were friends. While it is a rare case of a rampager knowing his victims, there is no evidence that Carneal intended to kill or maim Jenkins in particular. In years after the shooting, Carneal wrote letters to Jenkins.[59] In the letters he apologized to Jenkins, and she accepted his apologies. She forgave him.

Jenkins asked her attorneys and state officials to help her arrange and facilitate a meeting with Carneal. Prison and the other state officials went to great lengths to arrange the session and to keep Jenkins safe during the meeting. Neither Jenkins' nor any of Carneal's attorneys objected to the holding of the meeting. The attorneys hired a professional mediator to facilitate the session.[60] In addition to the mediator and Carneal and Jenkins, members of both families also attended. Significant was who was *not* present at the meeting. No attorneys, civil or criminal, prosecution or defense, attended; nor did any judge.

At the meeting Jenkins asked Carneal questions that burned in her mind for ten painful years. She also explained to him exactly how his .22-caliber bullet inextricably and profoundly altered her life forever, permanently paralyzing her from the waist down and forever confining her to a wheelchair. Jenkins asked him what his intentions were the morning of the rampage. According to Jenkins:

> He said that something inside him told him to carry out the shooting. He didn't know what it was, or why, but he just felt it was something he needed to do. And, as I expected, he didn't think of the consequences. He figured he would go to jail, he said, but the lives he might ruin never seemed to enter his mind.[61]

Still not satisfied, Jenkins pressed Carneal to answer the "why" question. According to Jenkins, "He said there really was no easy answer." After listening to Carneal's stories of how classmates at the high school treated him, she said, "bullying may have been part of it."[62] She also concluded that mental illness was a significant factor.

At the session, Carneal apologized to Jenkins. Although he had apologized in his letters, Jenkins felt "it was nice to hear him say it to [her] in person."[63] Jenkins was clear that, while the meeting did not provide her with all of the answers she sought, it was a valuable experience for her: "I've always said that there will never be closure for me. But I think that visit was the closest I'll ever come."[64]

Peter Lanza's Meetings with Newtown Victims

The Newtown-Lanza case further highlights the importance of an opportunity for victims to have a discourse with offenders or their families. In rampage killings where the rampager dies in the incident, gaining an understanding of the killer's motives is not very important to prosecuting attorneys. With no murder case to prosecute, motive is not the prosecutor's objective, and therefore, not a priority for the homicide detectives who investigate cases for prosecutors.

Determining motive in rampage murders is, however, of great interest to law enforcement, criminologists, and sociologists whose objective is to prevent future mass shootings. More important as it relates to the subject of this study, understanding motive is of great importance to surviving victims, family members, and the communities where mass shootings occur. People struggle to understand why innocent victims are killed or wounded. They want answers about how the crimes were committed. They also want to express their emotions to the killer or the killer's family. Allowing this expression to occur would help surviving family members gain closure.

Adam Lanza carefully planned his crimes. Still, he left behind no evidence of his motive. Lanza carefully studied the shootings at Columbine High School.[65] He would have been aware of the extensive evidence of motive that Eric Harris and Dylan Klebold left behind in diaries, on videos, and on websites. The lack of motive evidence left behind by Adam Lanza strongly suggest it was intentional.

Stephen J. Sedensky, the Danbury, Connecticut, prosecutor in charge of the Adam Lanza–Newtown investigation and prosecution summed up the lack of motive evidence:

The obvious question that remains is: "Why did the shooter murder twenty-seven people, including twenty children?" Unfortunately, that question may never be answered conclusively, despite the collection of extensive background information on the shooter through a multitude of interviews and other sources. The evidence clearly shows that the shooter planned his actions, including the taking of his own life, but there is no clear indication why he did so, or why he targeted Sandy Hook Elementary School.[66]

With Lanza dead, as is the case with the culprits of many rampage mass shootings, and with Lanza's guardian dead and no motive evidence forthcoming, some of the families of the victims sought the next best thing, a meeting with Lanza's estranged father, Peter Lanza.[67] The meetings did occur and they served a number of very valuable purposes.[68]

Peter Lanza had a desire to help the families of his son's rampage, and also to help prevent another similar horror. Lanza called the meetings "gut-wrenching." He said one family wanted to forgive Adam Lanza: "A victim's family told me that they forgave Adam after we spent three hours talking. . . . I didn't even know how to respond. A person that lost their son, their only son."[69]

One private meeting between Peter Lanza and Alissa and Robbie Parker, the parents of slain Emilie Parker, received substantial media coverage, including interviews of the parents on CBS News. Emilie Parker, six years old, was one of Adam Lanza's victims. Robbie Parker said that he and his wife wanted to meet with Peter Lanza because he was the only person who could answer their questions.[70]

About the meeting, the Parkers said they shared condolences. In contrast to many of the non-indigenous case studies reviewed in this book, the Parkers told Peter Lanza that they did not hold him, as a parent, responsible for their daughter's death. "I don't feel like he should be held responsible for what happened that day," said Alissa Parker.[71] "That was not ultimately his decision to do that, so how can I hold him responsible? Were there missteps in the raising of his son? Possibly." The Parkers viewed Nancy Lanza and Peter Lanza, and their respective accountability for the tragedy, quite differently.

> Peter and Nancy, in our minds, have to be held to different standards when we talk about blame or responsibility. One was directly involved in Adam's daily life [and] the other one was not. When Peter explained his relationship with Adam he did so without excuses. He was honest about their relationship and he wasn't trying to

shun his involvement in Adam's life in anyway. He was looking for answers he didn't have because of the estrangement of their relationship and this was something we felt very much affected Peter. . . . Also, Peter had the opportunity to tell us his side of the story. Nancy did not. We are not above realizing that it is easier to blame somebody that cannot defend themselves and that might play a small part in how we feel about both Peter and Nancy.[72]

The Parkers found the meeting they had with Peter Lanza to be productive for a number of reasons.

First, it allowed us to see Adam as a real human being and allowed at least some portion of empathy into our understanding of the entire situation.

It also allowed us to be at peace with the idea that there will be some answers that will simply not be known. We were also pleased to learn that Peter was working diligently to discover the answer to a lot of the same questions we all had after the tragedy. Even though he couldn't provide them, we felt he was doing what he could to make whatever could be known, known.

It also allowed for us to have empathy for what struggles he was facing. This event affected us so differently and it is very easy to become engulfed in what we had to face. I guess we were going through something that very few people could understand, and here we were talking to someone going through something we would never understand.[73]

For Alissa Parker there is a big difference between the role of Peter Lanza and the role of Nancy Lanza in her daughter's death. She holds Nancy Lanza partially responsible, as Adam's caregiver and the person who allowed him access to the weapons used to kill her daughter.[74] "Adam Lanza is solely responsible for his decisions. However, Nancy Lanza is responsible to her duties as a mother and provider for Adam's health and well-being. She is the one who best understood what her son struggled with and yet provided an environment that facilitated this tragedy."[75]

Alissa Parker held Adam Lanza responsible for her daughter's death, but she was mild in her criticism and took a religious approach to forgiveness, "I do hold him accountable, but I feel like God will determine that," she said. "And I feel like he's in a place where the judgment will happen, and I don't have to [be the one to make it]. I don't have to judge him, and I'm at peace with that."[76]

Alissa and Robbie Parker's willingness to meet with Peter Lanza, and their willingness to ultimately forgive Adam Lanza, were, no doubt, influenced by their religious beliefs.[77] As Alissa Parker said:

> Forgiveness is not an automatic response. Our religious upbringings taught us about forgiveness and allowed for us to have practiced forgiveness in our lives before this tragedy. In that way we had learned through experience the benefits of possessing a forgiving heart. The path to forgiveness, especially in a situation as this, is not easy and it is not ever fully complete. We still work on different aspects of forgiveness to this day.
>
> For example, we have to forgive Adam not just once but hundreds if not thousands of times a year. Every moment we share without [Emilie], birthdays, school days, family vacations, we have to forgive him for not knowing how to parent Madeline [Emilie's younger sister] better because we didn't get to experience those situations with Emilie first. In that way forgiveness is an ongoing process, not a one and done experience that many people try to portray. The attributes that are taught in a religious culture or household does allow for the attributes of empathy, patience and forgiveness to be understood and practiced in a way that we would not have had otherwise. We are, by no means, an example about how to forgive, because everyone will have to find their own path and journey to forgiveness. We are currently finding ours.[78]

At the time of his meeting with the Parkers, the statute of limitations was still running on possible civil suits, and the world watching closely, so Peter Lanza deserves a great deal of credit for participating in the victim meetings he attended.[79]

Rampage shootings continue to occur with great frequency in the United States. In fact, in the years since beginning research for this book, mass shootings continued to occur with startling frequency. One study counted seventy-four school shootings in the United States alone in the year and a half after the shootings in Sandy Hook, Connecticut. Several more occurred in 2015 and 2016.[80]

Evidence of Need for Healing Following Mass Shootings

For family members who have had a child, a parent, or a sibling die after a mass shooting, or any murder for that matter, methods for healing and the timing of these methods are very personal. Dr. Carolyn L. Mears is the parent of two children who survived the shootings at Columbine High School. She authored the book *Reclaiming School in the Aftermath of Trauma*.[81] She said that the repercussions from tragedies like the shootings at Sandy Hook Elementary School do not begin or end on any one day, but are part of an ongoing process.[82] "People want to know when they are going to heal, but there is no answer."[83]

Yet, as shootings have continued unabated, the desire for healing that follows mass shootings seems to be gaining momentum. Two developments evidence the desire for healing among the families described in this book: continued private meetings between the parents of the shooters and the parents of victims, and apologies from parents of shooters.

The 2013 meeting of Adam Lanza's father, Peter Lanza, with the parents of Emilie Parker, Robbie and Alissa Parker, was followed about a year later in 2014 with another private, and unofficial, historic meeting. On June 1, 2014, in advance of Father's Day, the father of Elliot Rodger met with the father of Christopher Martinez.[84]

Elliot Rodger is the twenty-two-year-old man who went on a shooting rampage May 23, 2014, in Isla Vista, California, a suburb of Los Angeles. In a delicatessen, Rodger shot and killed Christopher Martinez, a student at the University of California, Santa Barbara. He also killed three men in his apartment and two women outside a college sorority house, according to police, then drove wildly in a black BMW, shooting at and injuring pedestrians.[85]

About the meeting with Elliot Rodger's father, Peter Rodger, Christopher Martinez's father Richard Martinez said, "We plan to work together so other families such as ours will not suffer as ours have. This was a private conversation between grieving fathers who've reached common ground."[86] The positive experiences with face-to-face interactions between the families of rampage murderers and the families of victims bears adapting to future cases.

A Second Trend: Family Members of Rampage Killers Offering Apologies

The second development that evidences the desire for healing is that of a parent of a mass shooter making an immediate public statement expressing sadness and remorse for the atrocities committed by their child. On September 17, 2013, Aaron Alexis murdered twelve innocent people and wounded others at the Navy Yard in Washington, DC, before he died in a shootout with police.[87] The next day his mother, Cathleen Alexis, held an impromptu press conference in her apartment in the Bedford–Stuyvesant neighborhood of Brooklyn, New York.[88] In her living room and with clergy standing beside her, Alexis read a brief six-sentence statement and released an audio recording. She said:

> September 18, 2013. Our son, Aaron Alexis, has murdered twelve people and wounded several others. [pause] His actions have had a profound and everlasting effect on the families of the victims. I don't know why he did what he did, and I'll never be able to ask him why. Aaron is now in a place where he can no longer do harm to anyone, and for that I am glad.[89]

This brief and powerful statement, at a minimum was a testament that a mother, too, could not explain her son's horrible actions, that she identified with his victims, and that she preferred he was no longer alive to do more harm. Whether she was advised by attorneys, the clergy that stood with her, or only her own moral counsel, it is certain her voice was preferred to the silence that typically follows mass shootings.

Public statements offered as part of the healing process continue to be a very recent trend. Five days after the 2014 Marysville Pilchuck High School shootings, Jaylen Fryberg's American Indian tribe, the Tulalip Tribes, denounced Fryberg's actions: "Tulalip Tribes denounce the horrific actions of Jaylen Fryberg, who took the lives of two of his classmates and grievously injured three others. . . . It is our custom to come together in times of grief."[90] Notably, however, the Tulalip Tribes made a point to say that they held compassion for the grieving family of Fryberg.[91]

It is a natural development, as rampage murders continue to shock the country, and, indeed, the world, that the families of both rampagers and their victims seek each other out, as if some gravitational pull is drawing them together. Their coalescence emerges at a time when restorative justice practices have gained renewed attention. Having examined the historical roots of restorative practices in select indigenous cultures, the next chapter examines modern-day restorative practices in greater detail, proceeding with caution so as not to over-emphasize or over-romanticize an inconsistent history.

Restorative Justice and Therapeutic Jurisprudence Today

How Much Can Be Borrowed?

The indigenous dispute resolution practices discussed in the previous chapter are credited as an inspiration for a movement in Anglo-Western courts toward two trends, the modern-day restorative justice practices and therapeutic jurisdiction.[1]

How much of an influence in the current restorative justice movement can be attributed to history? A number of scholars influential in the restorative justice field have tried to make the link. For example, John Braithwaite, who is considered one of the world's foremost scholars on restorative justice, stated: "Restorative justice has been the dominant model of criminal justice throughout most of human history for all of the world's peoples."[2] Other scholars have gone further, elevating restorative justice to superior status as it compares to the modern punitive approach. Elmar G. M. Weitekamp wrote: "Forms of restorative justice, as we could find them in acephalous societies and especially early state societies, seem to be the better answer to the crime problem of today's societies."[3]

There is debate in the academic community whether the efforts by criminologists and criminal justice practitioners to document international traditions of restorative justice is entirely accurate.[4] At least two scholars believe restorative justice scholars have wandered into a danger zone, employing historical arguments to create an "origin myth."[5] One of these scholars is Kathleen Daly, a criminologist and restorative justice advocate.[6] Daly, critical of what she viewed as superficial and selective historical accounts, claimed that they have given restorative justice history a "pre-modern past [that] is romantically (and selectively) invoked to justify a current justice practice."[7] Daly believes this intellectual dishonesty is mistaken and may ultimately harm the acceptance of restorative justice, an outcome she views negatively.

Douglas Sylvester shares Daly's concerns. He said restorative justice scholars are "intent on minimizing the role that punitive processes, such as the 'blood feud' played in ancient cultures."[8] Indeed, this book, too, reveals examples in the historical record of indigenous peoples throughout the world who resorted to the use of punitive measures, even death under certain circumstances.

Sylvester went back and unearthed the research of scholars such as Weitekamp and E. Adamson Hoebel, and reviewed Hoebel's study, *The Law Of Primitive Man*.[9] Sylvester compared their research to their conclusions. "As it turns out," said Sylvester, "the restorative justice conclusion is either grossly overstated or flatly contradicted," when referring to Hoebel's conclusions.[10] Sylvester said the research of Hoebel and others, such as Laura Nader and Elaine Combs-Schilling, finds a restorative, victim-oriented and restitution-based approach to be common historically, but one that permitted violence and even death to an offender who failed to pay the determined restitution.[11]

Perhaps, then, the attempt to elevate restorative justice's historical link could well be fantasy. The fantasy is especially pernicious in law, as law desires to promote history as precedent for modern practice. "For lawyers," said Robert W. Gordon, "the past is primarily a source of authority—if we interpret it correctly, it will tell us how to conduct ourselves now."[12] Nonetheless, today's therapeutic jurisprudence recognizes that courts can play an important role in solving the underlying problems common to offenders and their families. These courts are often called "problem-solving courts," and they focus on problems like family dysfunction, addiction, delinquency, domestic violence, and mental health.[13] In problem-solving courts it is no longer enough for the courts to adjudicate facts and legal issues; their objective is to change future behavior and ensure the health and well-being of the community.[14]

Interest in restorative justice and therapeutic justice began to gain momentum in the 1970s and 1980s. The Navajo Nation in the United States created the Peacemaker Court in 1982.[15] By the 1990s restorative programs had spread to all Western countries, with at least seven hundred in Europe and three hundred in the United States.[16] The first problem-solving court in the United States was the Miami-Dade County Drug Court, established in the state of Florida in 1989. The court replaced prison and other traditional sanctions for drug-addicted offenders with judicially supervised treatment. Since 1989 several variations on the drug-court model emerged, including mental health courts, veterans' courts, homelessness courts, domestic violence courts, and community courts. By 2010, according to the National Drug Court Institute, more than 3,600 problem-solving courts were in operation in the United States.[17]

It makes good sense, then, that both restorative justice and therapeutic justice have taken root today. The prevalence of gun violence in the United States, whether a rampage at a school or a concert, a neighborhood gang-related drive-by shooting, or a fatal domestic violence tragedy, just to name a few, have contributed to "a growing sense of personal danger [and] a drastic deterioration of community fabric which breeds fear, isolation and estrangement from those who are different from us."[18] Mass incarceration and the modern Western reliance on punishment have led many scholars, like Professor Mark Umbreit at the University of Minnesota, to conclude that punishment alone, "seems to have made little progress, if any, in solving the levels of crime and violence."[19]

Accordingly, today there are three basic categories of restorative justice programs, depending on who runs the programs. There are private, community-based programs, church/religious institution programs, and criminal justice system–based programs.[20] From the 1970s to the 1980s, restorative justice programs were more popular with juvenile cases and adult misdemeanor cases than serious felonies. As the restorative-justice approach is now taking hold, though, it is beginning to be used in adult cases and occasionally in serious felony cases.[21] Today restorative justice programs throughout the world can be summarized in the following types: victim-offender mediation, community and family group conferencing, circle sentencing, and victim impact panels and surrogate groups.[22]

Victim-offender mediation is the most well developed and established type of restorative justice dialogue.[23] The goal of victim-offender mediation (sometimes called victim-offender reconciliation programs, or VORP) is to hold offenders accountable for their conduct while also providing for the possibility of assistance and compensation for victims. Victim-offender mediation gives victims, if they are interested, the opportunity to meet with offenders in a safe and structured environment. The process for victim-offender mediation is that, typically, a victim and offender enter into direct mediation, a dialogue facilitated by one or possibly two mediators/facilitators. Occasionally the dialogue takes place with the victim and offender in separate rooms, and the dialogue involves a third party who brings information from one party to the other. Today there are more than three hundred victim-offender mediation programs in the United States.[24]

An example of a victim-offender mediation program being used in felony cases is the one implemented in the Des Moines, Iowa, Polk County Attorney's Office. It was established in 1991 and referred to as VORP.[25] Since its inception the program conducted more than five thousand victim-offender mediations. This now includes as many felonies as non-felonies, with many burglaries, robberies, thefts, and forgeries included. Several murders, vehicular homicides, kidnaping, and sexual assault cases have been handled in the Polk County VORP.[26] In fact, domestic abuse assault cases are the only category of criminal cases excluded automatically in the Polk County VORP.[27] According to the Polk County Attorney's Office, 98 percent of VORP cases resulted in restitution agreements, 96 percent of VORP participants would choose to participate again in a VORP if they had the opportunity, and 86 percent of victims felt it was helpful to meet with their offender.[28]

Modern cases end up in restorative justice programs in a variety of ways. They can be sent to a VORP in lieu of or before an arrest is made, or following an arrest. They can be diverted to a program outside of the court system. Courts themselves may administer a restorative program and cases may be sent to a restorative program after a conviction but before sentencing. Restorative programs might be part of sentencing procedures.

Beginning in the early 1990s, the New York State court system embarked on a set of initiatives in a number of courts embodying both restorative and therapeutic justice themes.[29] The state created the Center for Court Innovation based on an experiment in Manhattan, New York, at the Midtown Community Court, which was created in 1993 to address minor street crime in the Times Square neighborhood. The Center for Court Innovation employs peacemaking principles in two courts in New York State, one in Brooklyn's Red Hook neighborhood and one in Syracuse. The center gives credit to indigenous peoples as an inspiration for its peacemaking programs:

> Through our relationships with tribal communities, where many restorative prac-
> tices originated, the Center for Court Innovation launched peacemaking programs
> in Red Hook and Syracuse. The Center supports community-led mediation and

violence prevention at the Crown Heights Mediation Center, and uses a peer-led and problem-solving approach to youth justice with its youth courts. We are also implementing school-wide restorative justice programs in five Brooklyn public high schools. Our research department will be evaluating the effectiveness of those programs, with a focus on disparities related to race and disability. The Center is committed to testing new restorative approaches to justice and shares lessons learned with jurisdictions around the world.[30]

Peacemaking is one of several programs operated by the Red Hook Community Justice Center, a multi-jurisdictional center combining traditional criminal, family, juvenile, and housing court functions. The Red Hook Peacemaking Program opened 132 new cases in 2016.[31] After its first six years, the justice center reported overall positive results both in offender compliance with alternative sanctions (75 percent compared to the 50 percent for urban courts nationwide) and offender perceptions of procedural fairness: more than 85 percent of criminal defendants believed their cases were handled fairly, and 93 percent agreed that the judge treated them fairly.[32]

Peacemaking in Red Hook, Brooklyn, is cited as the inspiration for another United States urban peacemaking-styled program, the Restorative Justice Community Court on the west side of the city of Chicago, Illinois. The program uses peace circles, bringing together the crime victim, community members, and court staff for a confidential conversation to discuss the incident. The community members collaborate on a legal agreement called a "repair of harm agreement."[33]

Restorative Justice among Indigenous Peoples Today

The Navajo Nation Peacemaking Program

In 1982 the Navajo Nation Peacemaking Program, which is based upon traditional Navajo methods of dispute resolution, was created by Navajo judges in judicial conference.[34] Today there are several types of peacemaking services in existence that are available through the Navajo Nation's courts. Traditional peacemaking (*hózhóji naat'aah*) is one such traditional service that may be obtained through the peacemaking program. If a court order is sought for a dispute, peacemaking may not be initiated for such a dispute. Such matters need to be filed first in court, and then referred to peacemaking programs by the court for all or part of the dispute.

The Navajo Peacemaking Participants

The Navajo Judicial Branch describes four types of participants in Navajo peace-making:

1. The peacemaker (*naat'áanii*) is an essential participant in the process. According to Robert Yazzie, the peacemaker is "a traditional Navajo civil leader whose authority comes from his or her selection by the community. The *naat'áanii* is chosen based on demonstrated abilities, wisdom, integrity, good character, and respect of the community."[35] The peacemaker acts as a guide, and everyone participating is treated as an equal.
2. The troubled individuals (*naałchidí*) are those confronting a chaos that disrupts inner and outer harmonious life, and who has agreed to the peacemaking process. "Children may be troubled together with family members when the family's combined decision is needed to change behaviors.[36]
3. The family members, workmates, friends, or others affected by the behavior of the troubled individual or knowledgeable about the chaos (*hóóchxo'/ anáhóót'i'*) also participate. These individuals may contribute to the talking-things-out process, but do not make the ultimate decision. They attend the peacemaking process with the permission of the group. Because of their presence and desire to contribute, they are called *atah naaldeehí*, or neutral intermediaries who help resolve the problem.[37]
4. The observers (*ha'a sí dí*). They attend the peacemaking process with the permission of the group, but do not speak.[38] Observers might be people training to be future peacemakers or might be attorneys and judges looking to learn more about peacemaking.

Traditional Navajo peacemaking begins in a place of chaos, whether existing within one person or between many. Navajos refer to the source of chaos as monsters (*naayéé'*), the things that prevent them from living a full life and result in disharmony.[39] Navajos typically avoid individual face-to-face confrontations. However, communal peacemaking seeks to find a way for people to air their grievances, as difficult as it may be.[40] The peacemaker has the skills and fortitude to provide the groundwork for the person or group to confront the chaos and move toward restoring relationships among those in conflict, and restoring relationships among families or within the clan. Engagement with the peacemaker provides the sense of identity and pride reaped from Navajo historical and cultural foundations.

Through engagement, the peacemaker scolds, educates, persuades, implores, pleads, and cajoles the individual or group toward an openness to listen, share, and make decisions together. Through stories and teachings, with the help of elders, the peacemaker dispenses wisdom in order to guide the person or group toward a restoration of relationships.

Apologies and the offering of forgiveness, elements of the paradigm suggested in the theoretical framework described by Thomas J. Scheff, R. D. Enright, and E. L. Worthington Jr. are important elements of the peacemaking process. The resolution of damaged feelings is the core material of peacemaking sessions. Depending on the skill of the peacemaker, the complexity of the problems, and the resistance of the offender or other participants, *hózhó* may be achieved quickly or may take several sessions.[41]

The Navajo Judicial Branch does not utilize formal peacemaking in murder cases, or subject them to the traditional restitution approach, in similar fashion to the Crow Dog case. The Navajo peacemaking model has spread to a vast array of indigenous peoples throughout the United States.[42] In addition to peacemaking, three other types of restorative programs are common today among indigenous peoples in the United States: talking circles, sentencing circles, and healing circles.

Talking Circles

A talking circle involves individuals sitting in a circle, taking turns expressing thoughts on an issue. In the circle, all participants have an equal place, just as in Navajo peacemaking. It is common for there to be a physical item, a "talking piece," that is used and passed around the circle. The talking piece can be a feather or another treasured object. Only the person holding the talking piece is allowed to speak. This process requires active and deep concentration and listening.

Historically, native cultures used talking circles as a way of bringing people together for the purposes of teaching, listening, and learning.[43] More recently, talking circles are being used to facilitate healing processes in both tribal and non-tribal communities.[44]

Sentencing Circles

According to the National Institute of Justice, "a sentencing circle is a community-directed process, conducted in partnership with the criminal justice system, to develop consensus on an appropriate sentencing plan that addresses the concerns of all interested parties."[45] A sentencing circle, which integrates tribal traditions and structure, occurs once someone has entered a guilty plea in an external court system. The use of sentencing circles began in the Yukon in the early 1980s and is now being regularly used in Minnesota.[46]

Healing Circles

One particular type of peacemaking circle is the healing circle. Separate healing circles may be held for the victim and the offender. The healing circle for the victim may be part of a larger circle process where both the victim and the offender will meet face to face in the same circle at a later date. On the other hand, the healing circle for the victim may be used entirely independent from the offender's circle. Furthermore, the healing circle may be the only process used in situations where the offender has not been identified or caught.

Here is a partial list of American Indian tribes utilizing some form of peacemaking:

- Arapaho Tribe of the Wind River Reservation, Wyoming
- Chickasaw Nation, Oklahoma
- Chitimacha Tribe, Louisiana
- Confederated Tribes of Siletz Indians, Oregon
- Confederated Tribes of the Colville Reservation, Washington
- Confederated Tribes of the Grand Ronde Community, Oregon
- Coquille Indian Tribe, Oregon
- Grand Traverse Band of Ottawa and Chippewa Indians, Michigan
- Ho-Chunk Nation, Wisconsin
- Hopland Band of Pomo Indians, California
- Kalispel Indian Community of the Kalispel Reservation, Montana
- Karuk Tribe, California
- Klamath Tribes, Oregon
- Leech Lake Band of Minnesota Chippewa Tribe, Minnesota

- Little River Band of Ottawa Indians, Michigan
- Little Traverse Bay Bands of Odawa Indians, Michigan
- Mashantucket Pequot Indian Tribe, Connecticut
- Mashpee Wampanoag, Massachusetts
- Mississippi Band of Choctaw Indians, Mississippi
- Navajo Nation, Arizona, New Mexico and Utah
- Oneida Nation, New York
- Oneida Tribe of Indians, Wisconsin
- Organized Village of Kake, Kansas
- Pit River Tribe, California
- Prairie Band Potawatomi Nation, Kansas
- Skokomish Indian Tribe, Washington
- Snoqualmie Indian Tribe, Washington
- Spirit Lake Tribe, North Dakota
- Stockbridge Munsee Community, Wisconsin
- White Earth Band of Chippewa, Minnesota[47]

Wellness and Healing Courts

Wellness courts, or what is often called "healing to wellness courts," have become widespread in American Indian communities, and is taking root outside these areas as well. "The institutionalization of healing to wellness courts suggests that a spiritual revolution swirls amid indigenous peoples and nations. Something stunningly spiritual is happening to indigenous North American jurisprudence,"[48] and it is a very noteworthy and favorable development. The tribes listed in appendix 2 are all operating some level of healing to wellness courts.

Other Examples of Healing within Existing Criminal Justice Systems

The Connecticut State Superior Court sentencing hearing of Chadwick St. Louis discussed in chapter 4 can be contrasted with some examples of restorative justice occurring around the world. One such example involving indigenous First Nation People of Canada is the case of a juvenile court hearing in British Columbia. The trial of an adult for murder is a very different and much more serious matter than a juvenile case of harassment, and both differ in scope from a mass murder. The offenses are not comparable. Still, an important lesson can be learned from the sentencing and how sentencing circles can work.

Dawn-Marie Wesley, fourteen years old and the daughter of an indigenous father, committed suicide in 2000.[49] She hung herself in the basement of her Mission, British Columbia, home with her dog's leash. Wesley wrote a suicide note where she said she could no longer take the bullying of three girls. One of the girls was convicted of criminally harassing Wesley.[50] The offender was a member of the Gitanmaax Band of First Nation People of Northwestern British Columbia.[51] Following a trial Wesley's mother, Cindy Wesley, requested a "sentencing circle." The participants in the sentencing circle were native elders, family members, court officials, and school officials.[52]

The sentencing circle was not held in a court room; it was held in a conference center. Over three long hours, twenty participants took turns speaking, each requesting to hold an eagle feather while speaking. Bill Bertschy of the Sliammon First Nation was the moderator, or "keeper of the circle."[53] He delivered the eagle feather to the participants. When it was the seventeen-year-old offender's turn to speak, twice she was unable to, crying too hard to speak. Finally, she took the hand of her grandfather, who was holding the feather, walked across the room to Cindy Wesley, and apologized to her: "I'm sorry for everything I have done to Dawn-Marie and your family."[54]

The judge, Provincial Court Judge Jill Rounthwaite, said she wanted the case to be used to help others and also to help the community make sure the offender did not offend again. "My hope is that all of us can work within our own family and with those children within our reach to help them understand that what they say off the cuff can be harmful and hateful," Rounthwaite said.[55] The offender was sentenced to eighteen months of probation, was ordered to speak to high school audiences about bullying, and to write a 750-word essay about bullying.

Cindy Wesley was pleased with the sentencing circle and the sentence. Most significantly, she credited it with allowing her to speak to one of the three offenders. She said that she got the healing she wanted and "the remorse [she] was looking for."[56] She compared it to the typical Western-style Anglo sentencing, saying that in a typical court hearing, "[one of the offenders] and I couldn't have talked."[57]

The desire to hear an expression of remorse, to speak to an offender or their family, and to have an interpersonal experience were common among the mass murder cases discussed in the Chadwick St. Louis sentencing. The British Columbia provincial sentencing circle achieved restorative and reconciliatory objectives. It also quite succinctly followed the theoretical forgiveness framework described by Thomas J. Scheff, R. D. Enright, and E. L. Worthington Jr.

New Zealand

Two significant findings were made in New Zealand by the 1980s with regard to criminal justice. One was recognition of the over-representation of Maori in the New Zealand prison system.[58] The second was an enhanced international recognition of the rights of indigenous peoples. Both contributed to a renewed interest in returning to Maori concepts of justice for the Maori people in New Zealand. Changes to the juvenile justice system in New Zealand incorporated many traditional Maori concepts for all offenders.[59] There was more resistance to changes for Maori adult offenders, which John Pratt attributes to a resistance to recognition of Maori sovereignty.[60]

A law was enacted in New Zealand in 1989 utilizing victim-offender mediation in juvenile offenses called "community conferencing," which is sometimes called family group conferencing.[61] The community conference is a diversion away from the courts to mediation. In Australia, community conferencing is now utilized in both juvenile and adult cases. It has been adopted in many other places around the world. It is worth noting that outside of indigenous communities, the restorative practices detailed in this book, with a few notable exceptions, have been limited largely to nonserious and misdemeanor offenses.[62]

How Much of Indigenous Practices Can Be Borrowed?

In suggesting that there are lessons to be gleaned from approaches among indigenous peoples to respond to rampage shootings, caution is advisable. The Anglo conceptions of forgiveness have been established as having their roots and influences in traditional Western religious beliefs such as Judaism and Christianity. A number of examples of community responses outside of indigenous communities further suggest that religious and spiritual beliefs impact the willingness to forgive and heal in the wake of horrific criminal actions. The responses in 2006 of the Amish of Nickel Mines, Pennsylvania, and the Parker family of Newtown, Connecticut, in 2012 are two such examples.[63]

At least one prominent scholar, Carole E. Goldberg, urges proceeding with caution in adopting native practices to non-native courts. Goldberg has taken note of the urge to import a number of American Indian tribal dispute resolution practices, including the invocation of tribal common law in court proceedings, referring disputes to elder panels and peacemaking, as alternatives to the traditional Western-style Anglo courts.[64] She referred to this urge as the potential for "over-extended borrowing."[65]

Peacemaking, as discussed throughout this book, is the most common indigenous dispute resolution method cited as a candidate for borrowing or appropriation. There are, no doubt, many obstacles for any non-indigenous culture that tries to adopt peacemaking.[66] As Angela Riley has pointed out, Navajo Nation peacemaking is "inherently 'religious' in that it draws on ceremony, prayer, ritual and the supernatural to restore balance, harmony and peace to the world."[67] The Navajo Blessingway Ceremony is one such traditional ceremony, or ritual, used to restore harmony. Adopting indigenous practices, which have a foundation in religious or spiritual beliefs, in non-indigenous cultures may run afoul of what Joseph Kalt and Stephen Cornell call the "cultural match."[68] Further, the Establishment clause of the First Amendment of the U.S. Constitution makes appropriation or borrowing of a strict Navajo-style peacemaking somewhat problematic.[69]

This book does not suggest, however, that a Navajo-style peacemaking, per se, is the solution to the treatment of rampagers, or their families. It does not hold out peacemaking or any other single indigenous practice as a roadmap toward forgiveness, reconciliation, and healing following heinous criminal offenses. Rather, it illuminates the dispute resolution practices that have existed among tribal people before adversarial Western-Anglo vertical systems existed.

I suggest here a role for filling an identified need among some victims of rampage murders and other heinous crimes. That need is for face-to-face, interpersonal encounters between victims and their families and offenders and their families. I identify practices of some indigenous cultures, historical and modern, along with modern select examples of non-indigenous peoples, such as the Amish, which have been more amenable to reconciliation.

I contrast those examples to the examples of finger pointing, blame seeking, and litigious conduct in non-indigenous cultures. Highlighted is the practice among non-indigenous peoples of the treatment of family members of offenders as pseudo-accomplices, a practice not common in the aftermath of the two American Indian tragedies studied. One cogent example of the contrasting aftermath is the resistance of non-indigenous communities to allow burial of rampage murderers in the community. In the American Indian cultures examined, as well as that of the Amish of Nickel Mines, Pennsylvania, the offenders were buried and memorialized with dignity.

A Time to Heal

Recommendations for a Way Forward

Integrating Healing and Restorative Justice Practices in the United States Criminal Justice System

Can face-to-face, interpersonal interactions between rampage murderers or their families and victims or their families result in reconciliation and greater healing in the days following rampage murders? Is there a role for government—whether it be the judiciary, the police, or other executive branch agencies—to play in facilitating or encouraging those interactions? Is there a role to play for non-governmental institutions?

A by-product of the adversarial system, particularly in the United States, is a wall of separation between offenders and their victims, who occasionally talk at each other in sentencing hearings in modern courtrooms, but hardly ever speak to one another. Another attribute of this system is that of "advised silence," where attorneys advise their clients not to utter a word, since, as the standard-issue Miranda card states, what they say "can and will" be used against their interests.

A dialogue and an interaction make possible understanding, confession, apology, forgiveness, and potentially reconciliation, and thus, in rampage murder cases where dialogue and interaction occur, cracks in the wall of separation are appearing.

The families of victims and offenders are seeking, on their own, interpersonal, face-to-face meetings—interactions—with one another. The meetings that are occurring are consistent with the research outlined here that says that forgiveness heals. Reconciliative interactions can be encouraged and facilitated by mental health providers and the psychiatric/psychological and counselling professionals who treat people harmed by rampage murders.

I have reviewed in previous chapters the rich history of dispute resolution among a sampling of indigenous peoples worldwide, which provides a long traditions of talking things out and community involvement in a dialogue between families of offenders and victims. Both restorative justice and the related therapeutic justice are beginning to appear in court systems around the world. Thus, we have long passed the point where dispute resolution is the only legitimate function served by criminal courts.

It is important, in closing, to turn our attention to specific recommendations for how restorative justice and lessons learned from indigenous peoples can be integrated into the U.S. criminal justice system and be applied as a healing approach to rampage murders.

Victim-Offender Healing Sessions

There are clear constitutional impediments to integrating a fully mandatory and binding restorative justice program in the United States, if participation is mandatory for the offender before adjudication of criminal charges or before the sentence is imposed. Mandatory offender participation at those stages is not permissible because it would violate a criminal defendant's right not to be "compelled in any criminal case to be a witness against himself," as the defendant is protected by the Fifth Amendment, and whose protection is extended to the states in the Fourteenth Amendment.[1]

Making participation mandatory in offender-victim meetings would be a violation of due process rights whenever jeopardy still exists. Procedural safeguards are required before the government can take a life, liberty, or property interest away from a person.[2] In *Mitchell v. United States*, the U.S. Supreme Court held that a defendant cannot be compelled to testify at a sentencing hearing, stating that "where the sentence has not yet been imposed a defendant may have a legitimate fear of adverse consequences from further testimony."[3] It also held that a sentencing court may not draw an adverse inference from a defendant's silence at the sentencing hearing in determining facts relating to the circumstances and details of the crime.[4]

When the objective of the proceedings is for healing to occur, according to Thomas J. Scheff's formula, both "symbolic reparations," and restoring the bonds between the offender and the community become important components. There is no constitutional impediment to mandatory participation of any person other than the offender. A valid concern, however, is any revictimizing of victims, who may suffer from reliving the horrors of a rampage and what it did to their lives, shattering their bodies and shattering their dreams. As with sentencing or parole hearings, their participation should be voluntary. One approach, which is suggested for increased victim participation in parole hearings, is to "borrow from psychology and develop interventions that will most likely help victims with the healing process, and subsequently with testifying."[5]

In those exceedingly rare cases where rampage murders do not result in the death of the offender, public safety concerns obviate diverting the case out of the criminal justice system. The rampage mass murder case is just too serious. The same goes for any intentional murder.[6] A healing session in the rampage mass murder case does not take the place of the fact-finding purpose of the criminal jury trial, nor does it replace the sentencing.

Healing Sessions Conducted before or after Sentencing

The following scheme could be adopted for serious cases, including rampage mass murders. Following a guilty plea, or a trial resulting in a conviction, the offender would be offered the option of participating in a voluntary healing session. It is imperative that this session be voluntary and not compelled. The session should be moderated by trained, expert facilitators—not prosecutors or judges. It should include victims and their families, and offenders and their families. Secure facilities would be required to ensure the safety of all participants.

A healing session could be conducted as part of the sentencing procedure so long as the offender's participation is not mandatory. When the session is conducted after adjudication but before sentencing, the facilitator would make findings that would be reported to the sentencing judge. The judge would decide whether to give any weight to what transpired in the session and whether it should affect the sentence in any way. A summary of the session could be incorporated in any sentencing report prepared for the judge.

Post-Sentencing Healing Sessions

The constitutional privilege against self-incrimination no longer exists once there is no longer a possibility of incrimination.[7] A U.S. federal court determines that the possibility of incrimination no longer exists "once the time for appeal has expired or until conviction has been affirmed on appeal."[8]

When is the ideal time for a healing session? Criminal cases are completed in less time than civil cases, but criminal appeals may not be exhausted for many years. If the case is a capital crime, that, in the case of a mass shooting, is certainly possible, appeals and habeas corpus proceedings may extend for decades. Civil suits and appeals take years to be resolved. An extension of some period of time after the tragedy may make for a more effective healing session. A session might be conducted years after the incident, and healing sessions held after the criminal sentencing has occurred are likely to be more effective after the offender has had a time of reflection. In the event of a child or young adult offender, the session may benefit from the period of time the offender has had to become more mature. The mental state of an offender might be improved after a period of mental health treatment and time have elapsed.

At a healing session family members of deceased victims would be allowed to speak, as would surviving injured victims. Family members of the offender would also be allowed to participate. Participants could direct questions to the offender. Once the jeopardy of self-incrimination no longer exists, the offender's participation could be made mandatory. A healing session that excludes the offender could be scheduled closer to the time of the offense than one that requires criminal or civil litigation to have been completed.

Some offenders might opt for participation in a healing session as part of their sentencing procedures if their participation is bargained for—they get something in return. A lack of sincerity by offenders is an obvious concern. Just as U.S. district court judges weigh the quality of cooperation with the government when giving credit in federal sentences for cooperation, expert healing session facilitators could report their assessment of offender sincerity to the sentencing judge.[9] A summary of what transpired in any healing session would be available for any judge considering an offender's subsequent and sentence-modification procedures or application for parole.

In order to make honest participation more likely, any statement made by any person in a healing session could be and should be made statutorily inadmissible

Timing of Litigation in the Heath High School Shooting

YEAR	CARNEAL'S AGE	YEARS SINCE OFFENSE	STAGE OF PROCEEDINGS
1997	14	0	Incident
1998	15	1	Criminal sentencing
2003	20	6	Civil litigation completed
2007	24	10	Healing session conducted
2008	26	11	Criminal appeals exhausted

in any future civil proceeding as well. The mental state of a living rampage mass murderer should be considered in deciding whether to and how to conduct a healing session. Just as mental health evaluations are conducted as part of many sentencing proceedings, evaluations should consider what the offender's participation in a healing session should be. Professionals should assess whether the offender could make a contribution to the session.

When the rampage mass shooter is not alive after the mass shooting, society would still benefit from the healing sessions or meetings among family members. Healing sessions would allow family members of offenders to meet with family members of victims, or victims themselves. The judiciary should be involved in arranging these sessions as well, since procedures and an infrastructure would be established for those sessions involving living offenders.

The model discussed above can be applied to rampage mass murder cases, some of which I discussed in earlier chapters. In fact, one rampage shooting case perfectly illustrates how a post-sentencing healing session might be conducted. Recall the case of Michael Carneal and the Heath High School shootings discussed in chapters 4 and 6. Carneal was just fourteen years old at the time of his murders. In 1998 he was sentenced to life in prison with the possibility of parole after twenty-five years. The civil litigation in the civil suits discussed in chapter 4 was resolved in 2003.[10] Although Carneal's criminal appeals were not completely exhausted until 2008, Carneal had a face-to-face prison meeting with one of his victims in 2007, ten years after the shooting. Carneal was diagnosed with paranoid schizophrenia.[11] While in prison, though, Carneal received treatment and medication.[12] The ten years following the shooting but preceding the healing session allowed Carneal to mature, get treatment, and reflect on his horrific offense. It also allowed Missy Jenkins, the victim, time to start physically and emotionally healing.

Jared Loughner, Tucson, Arizona

Jared Loughner murdered six people at a shopping center parking lot in Tucson, Arizona, on January 8, 2011.[13] He killed U.S. District Court Judge John Roll and five others, including nine-year-old Christina-Taylor Green.[14] Loughner wounded twelve others, including causing a permanent brain injury to U.S. congresswoman Gabrielle Giffords. Loughner pleaded guilty to nineteen counts in exchange for a life sentence. His plea provided no chance of parole or appeal. At his plea hearing, psychologist Dr. Christina Pietz, who treated Loughner at a federal hospital in Springfield, Missouri, said Loughner's feelings had evolved—from regret for failing to kill Ms. Giffords, whom he had harbored a secret grudge against for several years, to remorse for wounding her and others and for taking people's lives.[15] Pietz said Loughner once told her "I especially cried for the child" and that he "yelled a lot because it hurt so bad." She testified, reading from notes she had kept of their encounters.[16]

At his plea, or sentencing hearing, Loughner did not speak, though. Perhaps at a voluntary healing session, he would have echoed some of the sentiments he told the psychiatrist. At the sentencing hearing Loughner's mother, Amy Loughner, wept quietly in a corner of the courtroom. Is there a way to involve a mother like Amy Loughner in a healing session? Would she and Mark Kelly, the husband of Gabrielle Giffords, speak to one another? Why not?

On May 25, 2011, four months after the shooting, Loughner delivered an incoherent rant in the courtroom and the judge found him to be legally incompetent. Four months later at the plea hearing, Judge Larry A. Burns said Loughner was a "different person," finding him competent.[17] Gabrielle Giffords, as one surviving victim, experienced many years of rehabilitation and has a lifetime of rehabilitation ahead of her. It's time for Loughner to contemplate the enormity of his crimes and express his heartfelt sorrow to Giffords and to the families of his other victims. The harm he did cannot be undone. He could, however, make their lives a little bit better.

Treatment of the Offender's Family Members

One of the lessons of the Red Lake and Tulalip tribes is that the treatment of parents and family members of mass murderers as outcasts, social pariahs, and even accomplices should end. Parents of mass murderers suffer the remainder of their lives knowing the carnage their offspring rained upon a community. In cases where the mass murderer dies, the parents have the right to grieve. They have the right to bury their child or dispose of the body of their loved one as they see fit. They shouldn't have to escape the community to conduct secret funerals or burials in the cloak of darkness. Protesting burials or funerals punishes innocent family members. It, too, should end.

One lesson taken from the Jeffrey Weise case and the Red Lake Chippewa Indians is that legislative barriers to awarding governmental compensation to the families of offenders should be repealed. The family members of mass murderers do not meet the traditional statutory definitions of a crime victim. They are not direct victims but may be victims, nonetheless. Their compensation simply requires a new definition.[18] *Merriam-Webster* defines "victim" as "one that is acted on and usually adversely affected by a force or agent."[19] Peter Lanza could afford mental health treatment to process the implications of the pain and suffering his son caused, but when a parent cannot afford such treatment, why should society refuse to assist them? A father like Peter Lanza is a grieving parent, too. Moreover, the family members of mass murderers, family members of those murdered in such cases, and the first responders are "sufferers," or "casualties," of the mass murder. First responders carry the wounds of the horrors they experience upon entering and processing a mass murder scene. Police officers and emergency medical technicians responding to the warlike scenes at Columbine High School or Sandy Hook Elementary School experience considerable trauma.

Training of Lawyers

Traditional legal education is well suited to train lawyers for the adversarial vertical system of justice discussed in previous chapters. It is less suited to train lawyers to succeed in horizontal systems and accomplish the healing and talking things-out approach suggested in this book. Lawyers generally do not receive a great amount of training in counselling or in-depth interaction with clients.[20] Skills more commonly taught to future social workers or psychologists would benefit lawyers involved in mass murder cases. These skills include empathetic listening, evaluation, crisis intervention, and referral to experts.[21]

Unless they pursue a joint degree or substantial continuing education after law school, criminal lawyers do not receive training in mental health or mental illness. The subject is rarely taught to law students.[22] The spotlight on mass shootings certainly has put this subject on the radar screen for educators. Richard E. Redding, a scholar who has studied this phenomenon and recommends adding the subject of forensic mental health to the traditional law school curriculum, believes law students would be receptive to the addition of the subject.[23]

Mental health and mental illness could and should be further integrated into the traditional first-year substantive criminal law course. It could also be added as an upper-level elective course such as Criminal Law and Psychology or Forensic Mental Health.[24] Greater focus on the subject in American law schools is long overdue. Topics such as strategies or defenses for handling cases where mental illness is apparent and where competency to stand trial is reviewed are both worthy of inclusion into such courses. Mental illness and mental health issues in sentencing, too, are worthy of academic instruction. Training criminal lawyers to understand mental illness and mental health will better equip them for careers, and will establish greater receptivity to therapeutic and restorative justice in the American courts.

CONCLUSION

A dialogue and an interaction between victims or their families and offenders or their families make possible understanding, confession, apology, forgiveness, and potentially reconciliation, and thus, in rampage murder cases where dialogue and interaction occur, cracks in the wall of separation are appearing. The families of some victims and offenders are beginning to seek, on their own, interpersonal, face-to-face interactions. The meetings that are occurring are consistent with the research outlined in this book that says that forgiveness heals. Reconciliative interactions can be encouraged and facilitated by mental health providers and the psychiatric/psychological and counseling professionals who treat survivors harmed by rampage murders.

In the previous chapter, several possibilities were explored for integrating the healing process into the modern criminal court system, while still being consistent with American constitutional limitations. Following a rampage murder, steps can also be taken to reverse the practice of society demonizing the parents and family members of rampage killers, and reverse the treatment of them as outcasts, social pariahs, and even pseudo-accomplices. Parents of rampage murderers often share in the suffering. The recommendations made for mass murders equally apply to all serious crimes where physical and emotional wounds are inflicted.

The monumental and enduring task of figuring out how to end a seemingly endless repetition of the gruesome shedding of innocent blood is a steep and rugged mountain to climb. Substantial challenges persist to eradicating this task where conflicting attitudes exist toward regulation of guns within a constitutionally permissible framework. Add in the problems of near epidemic proportions facing (almost exclusively) men, and mostly young men who commit violence, of depression, suicide, mental illness, legal and illegal substance abuse, and the challenges to ending this task approach the insurmountable.

I leave for others and another day the facing of those challenges head on, figuring out how to make workplaces and schools safe again, and restoring serenity in houses of worship or any of the modern-day places people congregate. I do so, by no means out of a lack of interest, which is profound, but because what is explored here is something different and something receiving scarce attention elsewhere.

Jeremy Richman, the father of six-year-old Avielle Richman, murdered by Adam Lanza at the Sandy Hook Elementary School, said this:

> We would often hear people say, "I can't imagine what you're going through. I can't imagine how hard it must be. I can't imagine losing your child." And while we appreciated the sentiment, the fact was that they were imagining it. They were putting themselves into our shoes, for at least a second. And as hard and as horrible as it sounds, we need people to imagine what it is like. We need to empathize with each other, to walk a mile in each other's shoes. Without that imagination, we'll never change.[1]

Richman is right. We can only imagine the excruciating pain when innocent children, parents, or siblings are gunned down. Just as forgiveness is complex, so is any rational construction of the correct approach to the aftermath of rampage murders. The empathy suggested by Avielle Richman's father is not exclusive to the parents of an innocent child murdered. It is all encompassing. The pain radiates deeply, impacts many; empathy should be without limits.[2]

The range of emotions, from profound rage to the irreconcilable sadness, have existed throughout the human experience across time. Much has changed, though, in the United States and much of the world in social complexity and in dispute resolution. The adversarial system replaced existing systems throughout the world that were characterized by greater community participation and greater family interaction, which lead to the resolution of brutal crimes. Sadly, we know there will be another horrific, painful rampage shooting. When there is, rather than respond in haste and solely in hatred and anger, perhaps a page can be torn from history to give us a fresh understanding.

Fatal Victims in Select Mass Shootings

ere is a list of the victims who were killed in the four tragedies examined in great detail in chapters two and three. So much attention is given to the killers, here and in mass media coverage, that it is only fitting to at least pay tribute to some of the people whose lives were tragically ended.

Littleton, Colorado (Columbine High School)   April 20, 1997[1]

1. Cassie Bernall, 17   Student
2. Steven Curnow, 14   Student
3. Corey DePooter, 17   Student
4. Kelly Fleming, 16   Student
5. Matthew Kechter, 16   Student
6. Daniel Mauser, 15   Student
7. Daniel Rohrbough, 15   Student
8. William Sanders, 47   Teacher
9. Rachel Scott, 17   Student
10. Isaiah Shoels, 18   Student
11. John Tomlin, 16   Student

12.	Lauren Townsend, 18	Student
13.	Kyle Velasquez, 16	Student

Newtown, Connecticut (Sandy Hook Elementary School)   December 14, 2012[2]

1.	Charlotte Bacon, 6	Student
2.	Daniel Barden, 7	Student
3.	Rachel Davino, 29	Behavioral therapist
4.	Olivia Engel, 6	Student
5.	Josephine Gay, 7	Student
6.	Dylan Hockley, 6	Student
7.	Dawn Hochsprung, 47	School principal
8.	Madeleine Hsu, 6	Student
9.	Catherine Hubbard, 6	Student
10.	Chase Kowalski, 7	Student
11.	Nancy Lanza, 52	Mother of shooter
12.	Jesse Lewis, 6	Student
13.	Ana Marquez-Greene, 6	Student
14.	James Mattioli, 6	Student
15.	Grace McDonnell, 7	Student
16.	Anne Marie Murphy, 52	Teacher
17.	Emilie Parker, 6	Student
18.	Jack Pinto, 6	Student
19.	Noah Pozner, 6	Student
20.	Caroline Previdi, 6	Student
21.	Jessica Rekos, 6	Student
22.	Avielle Richman, 6	Student
23.	Lauren Rousseau, 30	Teacher
24.	Mary Sherlach, 56	School psychologist
25.	Victoria Soto, 27	Teacher
26.	Benjamin Wheeler, 6	Student
27.	Allison Wyatt, 6	Student

Blacksburg, Virginia (Virginia Tech University)   April 16, 2007[3]

1.	Ross Alameddine, 20	Student

2. Jamie Bishop, 35   Professor
3. Brian Bluhm, 25   Student
4. Ryan Clark, 22   Student
5. Austin Cloyd, 18   Student
6. Jocelyn Couture-Nowak, 49   Professor
7. Kevin Granata, 45   Professor
8. Matthew Gwaltney, 24   Student
9. Caitlin Hammaren, 19   Student
10. Jeremy Herbstritt, 27   Student
11. Rachael Hill, 18   Student
12. Emily Hilscher, 19   Student
13. Jarrett Lane, 22   Student
14. Matthew La Porte, 20   Student
15. Henry Lee, 20   Student
16. Liviu Librescu, 76   Professor
17. G. V. Loganathan, 53   Professor
18. Partahi Lumbantoruan, 34   Student
19. Lauren McCain, 20   Student
20. Daniel O'Neil, 22   Student
21. Juan Ortiz, 26   Student
22. Minal Panchal, 26   Student
23. Daniel Perez Cueva, 21   Student
24. Erin Peterson, 18   Student
25. Michael Pohle Jr., 23   Student
26. Julia Pryde, 23   Student
27. Mary Karen Read, 19   Student
28. Reema Samaha, 18   Student
29. Waleed Shaalan, 32   Student
30. Leslie Sherman, 20   Student
31. Maxine Turner, 22   Student
32. Nicole White, 20   Student

Red Lake, Minnesota (Red Lake High School)   March 21, 2005[4]

1. Derrick Brun, 28   School security guard
2. Dewayne Lewis, 15   Student

3. Chase Lussier, 15   Student
4. Daryl Lussier, 59   Grandfather of shooter
5. Neva Rogers, 62   Teacher
6. Chanelle Rosebear, 15   Student
7. Michelle Sigana, 31   Girlfriend of shooter's grandfather
8. Thurlene Stillday, 15   Student
9. Alicia White, 14   Student

Mass Shootings in the United States, 1982–2018

R ampage shootings occur in the United States at a disturbing rate. Some rampages are well known to the public, while many others are only known in the locality where they occurred. My hope is that including the list here will help put the crisis into perspective and will be useful as a resource. The list is nowhere near complete but includes mass shootings committed in the United States from 1982–2018. Up until 2015 the Federal Bureau of Investigation (FBI) and many criminologists, like Robert Hazelwood and John Douglas, classified "mass shootings" as those where at least four victims were killed. In January 2013 the FBI changed its classification to include rampages where at least three victims were killed, so this list includes them as well, from 2013–2018. I relied on the compilation done by *Mother Jones*, a database they began to keep and update in 2012 after the tragedy at the Aurora, Colorado, movie theater. The *Mother Jones* compilation, and thus this list, only includes murders occurring in public places (so, does not domestic violence, for example) does not include mass murders involving other more common street crime, such as robberies or gang violence.[1]

Mercy Hospital shooting

■ **CHICAGO, IL**   11/19/2018   **JUAN LOPEZ, 32**

Lopez confronted his former fiancée at the ER, killing her and two others, including a police officer. Lopez, who had a history of domestic violence, was killed by responding police.

Thousand Oaks nightclub shooting

■ **THOUSAND OAKS, CA**   11/17/2018   **IAN D. LONG, 28**

Long, a former marine, entered the Borderline Bar and Grill, a country music venue, and opened fire, killing twelve and injuring twenty-two with a handgun.

Tree of Life synagogue shooting

■ **PITTSBURGH, PA**   10/27/2018   **ROBERT D. BOWERS, 46**

Bowers entered the synagogue during Sabbath morning services, shouting anti-Semitic slurs. He opened fire with an assault rifle and multiple handguns, killing eleven and injuring six. His social media posts were filled with virulent anti-Semitic and racist content. He was arrested and faces charges in U.S. federal court.

Rite Aid warehouse shooting

■ **PERRYMAN, MD**   9/20/2018   **SNOCHIA MOSELEY, 26**

Moseley, a temporary employee, shot fellow employees inside the distribution center, killing three and injuring three more. She died later that day of a self-inflicted gunshot.

T&T Trucking shooting

■ **BAKERSFIELD, CA**   9/12/2018   **JAVIER CASAREZ, 54**

Going through a bitter divorce, Casarez took his ex-wife to the trucking company where, with a handgun he killed her and two coworkers. He killed others at two other locations. He carjacked a woman and her son before letting them go, and then fatally shot himself as police were closing in on him.

Fifth Third Center shooting

■ **CINCINNATI, OH**   9/6/2018   **OMAR E. SANTA PEREZ, 29**

Perez walked into the lobby of a building in downtown Cincinnati and opened fire with a handgun. He killed three and wounded two before dying in a shootout with responding police.

Capital Gazette shooting

■ **ANNAPOLIS, MD**   **6/28/2018**   **JARROD W. RAMOS, 38**

Ramos had a longstanding grudge against the newspaper since it published a 2011 column reporting on his guilty plea for the harassment of a former female classmate. With a shotgun he shot his way through the glass doors of the newsroom, killing five and injuring two. He was captured alive in the news room.

Santa Fe High School shooting

■ **SANTA FE, NM**   **5/18/2018**   **DIMITRIOS PAGOURTZIS, 170**

With a shotgun and .38-caliber revolver seventeen-year-old Pagourtzis, a student, opened fire at Santa Fe High School, killing ten and injuring thirteen more before surrendering to the police after a standoff and additional gunfire in the school.

Waffle House shooting

■ **NASHVILLE, TN**   **4/22/2018**   **TRAVIS REINKING, 29**

With a history of erratic behavior and run-ins with police in Illinois, Reinking, armed with an AR-15, opened fire at around 3:30 a.m. in the parking lot of a Waffle House. He continued shooting in the restaurant, killing four and wounding four others.

Yountville veterans home shooting

■ **YOUNTVILLE, CA**   **3/9/2018**   **ALBERT C. WONG, 36**

U.S. Army veteran Wong, who served in Afghanistan and had a history of PTSD, stormed into the veterans' home where he was previously a patient and was expelled for threatening behavior.[2] He took three staff women hostage and exchanged gunfire with a sheriff's deputy. After a standoff with the police and armed with a rifle he killed the three women and himself.

Marjory Stoneman Douglas High School shooting

■ **PARKLAND, FL**   **2/14/2018**   **NIKOLAS J. CRUZ, 19**

Cruz, a nineteen-year-old with a history of behavioral problems, attacked the high school as classes were ending for the day. Heavily armed with an AR-15, tactical gear, and countless magazines of ammo, he killed seventeen people and wounded seventeen more. He was captured alive by police shortly after fleeing the campus.

Pennsylvania carwash shooting spree

■ **MELCROFT, PA**   **1/18/2018**   **TIMOTHY O. SMITH, 28**

Early in the morning Smith went to a carwash in the rural community to confront twenty-five-year-old Chelsie Cline, who had recently broken up with him. Wearing body armor and heavily armed with a rifle and much ammunition he opened fire, killing Cline and four others. Later that night, Smith succumbed to a fatal self-inflicted shot to his head.

Rancho Tehama school shooting

■ **RANCHO TEHAMA, CA**   **11/14/2017**   **KEVIN J. NEAL, 44**

Armed with two rifles, Neal first killed his wife at her rural Northern California home. He continued a forty-five-minute shooting spree, killing a woman who had a protective order against him, then shooting up an elementary school. He killed a total of five people and injured ten before being killed by responding police.

Texas First Baptist Church massacre

■ **SUTHERLAND SPRINGS, TX** **11/5/2017**   **DEVIN P. KELLEY, 26**

Armed with a rifle, Kelley, a former U.S. Air Force airman who had a history of domestic violence, opened fire at the First Baptist Church in Sutherland Springs during Sunday morning services. He killed twenty-six people and injured another twenty before fleeing in his car, and engaging in a gun-fight with a civilian. He crashed his car and died from a self-inflicted gunshot wound.

Walmart shooting in suburban Denver

■ **THORNTON, CO**   **11/1/2017**   **SCOTT A. OSTREM, 47**

Ostrem, a metal worker, quit his job and then the next day walked into a Walmart in a suburb north of Denver with a handgun. He killed three people before driving away. He was captured by the police after being located near his Denver apartment.

Edgewood business park shooting

■ **EDGEWOOD, MD**   **10/18/2017**   **RADEE L. PRINCE, 37**

Prince went to his workplace, Advance Granite Solutions, at around 9:00 a.m. Armed with a handgun, he killed three people and injured two others. He then went to a car dealership in Wilmington, Delaware, where he wounded a third person. He was captured by police that evening following a manhunt.

Las Vegas concert massacre

■ **LAS VEGAS, NV**   10/1/2017   **STEPHEN C. PADDOCK, 64**

Paddock positioned himself in a corner suite on the thirty-second floor of the Mandalay Bay Resort and Casino, on the Las Vegas resort strip. Late on a Sunday night he fired down at a massive crowd of concertgoers below. He unleashed a barrage of rapid gunfire from broken out windows of the hotel, with semiautomatic rifles modified with bump stocks. Paddock killed fifty-eight people and wounded 546 more before police managed to get into his hotel room, where they found him dead from a self-inflicted gunshot and with an arsenal of twenty-three firearms.

San Francisco UPS shooting

■ **SAN FRANCISCO, CA**   6/14/2017   **JIMMY LAM, 38**

Lam, who worked in a UPS facility in San Francisco, killed three coworkers there and wounded two others. Armed with two handguns, he killed himself as police responded to the scene.

Pennsylvania supermarket shooting

■ **TUNKHANNOCK, PA**   6/7/2017   **RANDY STAIR, 24**

Stair, a worker at Weis grocery store, fatally shot three of his fellow employees at work. He fired fifty-nine rounds with a pair of shotguns before turning the gun on himself as police responded.

Florida awning manufacturer shooting

■ **ORLANDO, FL**   6/5/2017   **JOHN R. NEUMANN JR., 45**

Neumann was a former employee of Fiamma Inc., which manufactures awnings for RVs, who had been recently fired. He went to the workplace and, armed with a handgun, killed five workers there before killing himself at the scene.

Rural Ohio nursing home shooting

■ **KIRKERSVILLE, OH**   5/12/2017   **THOMAS HARTLESS, 43**

Hartless had a history of violence, and his former girlfriend had recently obtained a court protection order against him. Armed with a shotgun and a handgun, he went to the nursing home where she worked and then shot and killed her and one of her coworkers, along with the Kirkersville police chief who responded to the scene. Hartless died at the scene of a self-inflicted shot. Police found an arsenal of more than sixty firearms at his home.

Fresno downtown shooting

■ **FRESNO, CA**   **4/18/2017**   **KORI A. MUHAMMAD, 39**

Muhammad opened fire with a handgun along a street in downtown Fresno, killing three people before being captured by police. Muhammad, who is black, killed three white victims and later described his attack as being racially motivated.

Fort Lauderdale airport shooting

■ **FORT LAUDERDALE, FL**   **1/6/2017**   **ESTEBAN SANTIAGO, 26**

Santiago flew from Alaska to Fort Lauderdale, where he opened fire with a handgun in the baggage claim area of the airport. He killed five and wounded six people before police captured him.

Cascade Mall shooting

■ **BURLINGTON, WA**   **9/23/2016**   **ARCAN CETIN, 20**

Cetin went to the cosmetics section of Macy's department store at the Cascade Mall, where, armed with a rifle, he killed a teenage girl and three other women. A fifth victim died later from wounds he had suffered at the shooting.

Baton Rouge police shooting

■ **BATON ROUGE, LA**   **7/17/2016**   **GAVIN LONG, 29**

Long was a former U.S. Marine who served in Iraq. He had expressed admiration on social media for Micah X. Johnson, who killed a police officer in Dallas ten days prior. Armed with two rifles and a handgun, Long killed three police officers who responded to a 911 call and wounded three others. Long was killed in a shoot-out with other police officers responding to the scene.

Dallas police shooting

■ **DALLAS, TX**   **7/7/2016**   **MICAH X. JOHNSON, 25**

Johnson was a former U.S. Army soldier. Armed with a rifle and handguns he targeted police officers at a peaceful Black Lives Matter protest, where he killed five police officers and and wounded nine other officers, along with wounding two civilians. After a prolonged standoff in a downtown building, police killed Johnson using a robot-delivered bomb.

Orlando nightclub mass shooting

■ ORLANDO, FL   6/12/2016   OMAR MATEEN, 29

Mateen, a private security guard, opened fire in crowded gay night club after pledging allegiance to ISIS.

Excel Industries mass shooting

■ HESSTON, KS   2/25/2016   CEDRIC L. FORD, 38

Ford, who worked as a painter at a manufacturing company, shot victims from his car and at his workplace before being killed by police at the scene. Shortly before the rampage he had been served with a restraining order.

Uber driver shooting spree

■ KALAMAZOO COUNTY, MI   2/20/2016   JASON B. DALTON, 45

Dalton, a driver for Uber, apparently selected his victims randomly as he went on a rampage over several hours in three different locations, including five people he shot in the parking lot of a Cracker Barrel restaurant. He was "arrested without incident" at a downtown Kalamazoo bar about six hours after the rampage began.

San Bernardino mass shooting

■ SAN BERNARDINO, CA   12/2/2015   SYED R. FAROOK, 28

Farook left a Christmas party held at Inland Regional Center, later returning with Tashfeen Malik, and the two opened fire, killing fourteen and wounding twenty-one, ten critically. The two were later killed by police as they fled in an SUV.

Planned Parenthood clinic shooting

■ COLORADO SPRINGS, CO   11/27/2015   ROBERT L. DEAR, 57

Dear shot and killed a police officer and two citizens when he opened fire at a Planned Parenthood health clinic in Colorado Springs, Colorado. Nine others were wounded. Dear was arrested after an hours-long standoff with police.

Colorado Springs shooting rampage

■ COLORADO SPRINGS, CO   10/31/2015   NOAH HARPHAM, 33

Harpham shot three people dead in Colorado Springs before police killed him in a shootout.

Umpqua Community College shooting

■ **ROSEBURG, OR**   **10/1/2015**   **CHRIS H. MERCER, 26**

Mercer opened fire at Umpqua Community College in southwest Oregon. The gunman shot himself to death after being wounded in a shootout with police.

Chattanooga military recruitment center

■ **CHATTANOOGA, TN**   **7/16/2015**   **MOHAMMOD Y. ABDULAZEEZ, 24**

Abdulazeez, Kuwaiti-born, a naturalized US citizen, opened fire at a Naval reserve center, and then drove to a military recruitment office where he shot and killed four marines and a navy service member, and wounded a police officer and another military service member. He was then fatally shot in an exchange of gunfire with law enforcement officers responding to the attack.

Charleston Church shooting

■ **CHARLESTON, SC**   **6/17/2015**   **DYLANN S. ROOF, 21**

Roof shot and killed nine people after opening fire at the Emanuel AME Church in Charleston, South Carolina. According to a roommate, he had allegedly been "planning something like that for six months."

Trestle Trail bridge shooting

■ **MENASHA, WI**   **6/11/2015**   **SERGIO V. DEL TORO, 27**

Del Toro, in what officials say was a random act, shot and killed three people including an eleven-year-old girl before turning the gun on himself.

Marysville Pilchuck High School shooting

■ **MARYSVILLE, WA**   **10/24/2014**   **JAYLEN FRYBERG, 15**

Fryberg, using a .40-caliber Beretta, shot five students at Marysville High School, including two of his cousins and three friends, killing all but one. Fryberg arranged to meet them for lunch in the school cafeteria by text. Fryberg was reportedly well-liked at the school, and there was not believed to be any ill-will between him and his victims. He committed suicide at the scene.

Isla Vista mass murder

■ **ISLA VISTA, CA**   **5/23/2014**   **ELLIOT RODGER, 22**

Rodger shot three people to death in the college town of Isla Vista near the University of California, Santa Barbara. He also shot others as he drove around town, and injured others by striking them with is vehicle. He committed suicide by shooting himself in his car as police closed in. Prior to the rampage, Rodger stabbed three people to death at his apartment.

Fort Hood shooting

■ **FORT HOOD, TX**   4/3/2014   **IVAN LOPEZ, 34**

Lopez, army specialist, opened fire at the Fort Hood army post, killing three and wounding at least twelve others before shooting himself in the head after engaging with military police. Lt. Gen. Mark A. Milley told reporters that Lopez "had behavioral health and mental health" issues.

Alturas tribal shooting

■ **ALTURAS, CA**   2/20/2014   **CHERIE LASH RHOADES, 44**

Rhoades opened fire at the Cedarville Rancheria Tribal Office and Community Center, killing four and wounding two. After running out of ammunition, Rhoades grabbed a butcher knife and stabbed another person.

Washington Navy Yard shooting

■ **WASHINGTON, DC**   9/16/2013   **AARON ALEXIS, 34**

Alexis, a military veteran and contractor from Texas, opened fire in the navy installation, killing twelve people and wounding eight before being shot dead by police.

Hialeah apartment shooting

■ **HIALEAH, FL**   7/26/2013   **PEDRO VARGAS, 42**

Vargas set fire to his apartment, killed six people in the complex, and held another two hostage at gunpoint before a SWAT team stormed the building and fatally shot him.

Santa Monica rampage

■ **SANTA MONICA, CA**   6/7/2013   **JOHN ZAWAHRI, 23**

Zawahri, armed with a homemade assault rifle and high-capacity magazines, killed his brother and father at home and then headed to Santa Monica College, where he was eventually killed by police.

Pinewood Village apartment shooting

■ **FEDERAL WAY, WA**   4/21/2013   **DENNIS CLARK III, 27**

Clark shot and killed his girlfriend in their shared apartment, and then shot two witnesses in the building's parking lot and a third victim in another apartment, before being killed by police.

Mohawk Valley shootings

■ **HERKIMER COUNTY, NY**   3/13/2013   **KURT MYERS, 64**

Myers shot six people in neighboring towns, killing two in a barbershop and two at a car care business, before being killed by officers in a shootout after a nearly nineteen-hour standoff.

Newtown school shooting

■ **NEWTOWN, CT**   12/14/2012   **ADAM LANZA, 20**

Lanza shot his mother dead at their home then drove to Sandy Hook Elementary School. He forced his way inside and opened fire, killing twenty children and six adults before committing suicide.

Accent Signage Systems shooting

■ **MINNEAPOLIS, MN**   9/27/2012   **ANDREW ENGELDINGER, 36**

Engeldinger, upon learning he was being fired, went on a shooting rampage, killing the business owner, three fellow employees, and a UPS driver. He then killed himself.

Sikh temple shooting

■ **OAK CREEK, WI**   8/5/2012   **WADE M. PAGE, 40**

Page, a U.S. Army veteran, opened fire in a Sikh gurdwara before he died from a self-inflicted gunshot wound during a shootout with police.

Aurora theater shooting

■ **AURORA, CO**   7/20/2012   **JAMES HOLMES, 24**

Holmes opened fire in a movie theater during the opening night of *The Dark Knight Rises* and was later arrested outside.

Seattle cafe shooting

■ **SEATTLE, WA**   **5/20/2012**   **IAN STAWICKI, 40**

Stawicki gunned down four patrons at a cafe and another person during a carjacking nearby, then shot himself as police closed in. (He died later that day in a Seattle hospital.)

Oikos University killings

■ **OAKLAND, CA**   **4/2/2012**   **ONE L. GOH, 43**

Goh, a former student, opened fire in a nursing classroom. He fled the scene by car and was arrested nearby a few hours later.

Su Jung Health Sauna shooting

■ **NORCROSS, GA**   **2/22/2012**   **JEONG S. PAEK, 59**

Paek returned to a Korean spa from which he'd been kicked out after an altercation. He gunned down two of his sisters and their husbands before committing suicide.

Seal Beach shooting

■ **SEAL BEACH, CA**   **10/14/2011**   **SCOTT E DEKRAAI, 42**

Dekraai opened fire inside a hair salon and was later arrested.

IHOP shooting

■ **CARSON CITY, NV**   **9/6/2011**   **EDUARDO SENCION, 32**

Sencion opened fire at an International House of Pancakes restaurant and later died from a self-inflicted gunshot wound.

Congress on Your Corner shooting

■ **TUCSON, AZ**   **1/8/2011**   **JARED LOUGHNER, 22**

Loughner opened fire outside a Safeway during a constituent meeting with Congresswoman Gabrielle Giffords (D-Ariz.) before he was subdued by bystanders and arrested.

Hartford Beer Distributors shooting

■ **MANCHESTER, CT**   **8/3/2010**   **OMAR S. THORNTON, 34**

Thornton shot up his Hartford Distributors workplace after facing disciplinary issues, then committed suicide.

Coffee shop police killings

■ **PARKLAND, WA**   **11/29/2009**   **MAURICE CLEMMONS, 37**

Clemmons, a felon who was out on bail for child-rape charges, entered a coffee shop on a Sunday morning and shot four police officers who had gone there to use their laptops before their shifts. Clemmons, who was wounded fleeing the scene, was later shot dead by a police officer in Seattle after a two-day manhunt.

Fort Hood massacre

■ **FORT HOOD, TX**   **11/5/2009**   **NIDAL M. HASAN, 39**

Hasan, an army psychiatrist, opened fire on an army base in an attack linked to Islamist extremism. Hasan was injured during the attack and later arrested.

Binghamton shootings

■ **BINGHAMTON, NY**   **4/3/2009**   **JIVERLY WONG, 41**

Wong opened fire at an American Civic Association center for immigrants before committing suicide.

Carthage nursing home shooting

■ **CARTHAGE, NC**   **3/29/2009**   **ROBERT STEWART, 45**

Stewart opened fire at a nursing home where his estranged wife worked before he was shot and arrested by a police officer.

Atlantis Plastics shooting

■ **HENDERSON, KY**   **6/25/2008**   **WESLEY N. HIGDON, 25**

Higdon, a disgruntled employee, shot up an Atlantis Plastics factory after he was escorted out of his workplace for an argument with a supervisor. Higdon shot the supervisor outside the factory before opening fire on coworkers inside. He then committed suicide.

Northern Illinois University shooting

■ **DEKALB, IL**   **2/14/2008**   **STEVEN KAZMIERCZAK, 27**

Kazmierczak opened fire in a lecture hall, then shot and killed himself before police arrived.

Kirkwood City Council shooting
■ **KIRKWOOD, MO**   **2/7/2008**   **CHARLES "COOKIE" L. THORNTON, 52**

Thornton went on a rampage at the city hall before being shot and killed by police.

Westroads Mall shooting
■ **OMAHA, NE**   **12/5/2007**   **ROBERT A. HAWKINS, 19**

Hawkins opened fire inside Westroads Mall before committing suicide.

Crandon shooting
■ **CRANDON, WI**   **10/7/2007**   **TYLER PETERSON, 20**

Peterson, off-duty sheriff's deputy, opened fire inside an apartment after an argument at a homecoming party. He fled the scene and later committed suicide.

Virginia Tech massacre
■ **BLACKSBURG, VA**   **4/16/2007**   **SEUNG-HUI CHO, 23**

Cho, Virginia Tech student, opened fire on his school's campus before committing suicide.

Trolley Square shooting
■ **SALT LAKE CITY, UT**   **2/12/2007**   **SULEJMAN TALOVIĆ, 18**

Talović rampaged through the shopping center until he was shot dead by police.

Amish school shooting
■ **LANCASTER COUNTY, PA**   **10/2/2006**   **CHARLES C. ROBERTS, 32**

Roberts shot ten young girls in a one-room schoolhouse in Bart Township, killing five, before taking his own life.

Capitol Hill massacre
■ **SEATTLE, WA**   **3/25/2006**   **KYLE A. HUFF, 28**

Huff opened fire at a rave after-party in the Capitol Hill neighborhood of Seattle before committing suicide.

Goleta postal shootings

■ **GOLETA, CA**   **1/30/2006**   **JENNIFER SANMARCO, 44**

Sanmarco, a former postal worker, shot dead a former neighbor then drove to the mail processing plant where she used to work. Inside, she opened fire, killing six employees before committing suicide.

Red Lake High School massacre

■ **RED LAKE, MN**   **3/21/2005**   **JEFFREY WEISE, 16**

Weise murdered his grandfather, who was a tribal police officer, and his grandfather's girlfriend. Weise then drove his grandfather's squad car to Red Lake High School and opened fire on the reservation campus, killing another seven people before committing suicide.

Living Church of God shooting

■ **BROOKFIELD, WI**   **3/12/2005**   **TERRY M. RATZMANN, 44**

Ratzmann, a Living Church of God member, opened fire at a church meeting at a Sheraton hotel before committing suicide.

Damageplan show shooting

■ **COLUMBUS, OH**   **12/8/2004**   **NATHAN GALE, 25**

Gale, possibly upset about the breakup of Pantera, gunned down former Pantera guitarist Dimebag Darrell and three others at a Damageplan show before a police officer fatally shot Gale.

Lockheed Martin shooting

■ **MERIDIAN, MS**   **7/8/2003**   **DOUGLAS WILLIAMS, 48**

Williams, an assembly-line worker, opened fire at his Lockheed Martin workplace in a racially motivated attack before committing suicide.

Navistar shooting

■ **MELROSE PARK, IL**   **2/5/2001**   **WILLIAM D. BAKER, 66**

Baker, a fired employee, opened fire at his former Navistar workplace before committing suicide.

Wakefield massacre

■ **WAKEFIELD, MA**   **12/26/2000**   **MICHAEL MCDERMOTT, 42**

McDermott opened fire on coworkers at Edgewater Technology and was later arrested.

Hotel shooting

■ **TAMPA, FL**   **12/30/1999**   **SILVIO LEYVA, 36**

Leyva, a hotel employee, gunned down four coworkers at the Radisson Bay Harbor Inn before killing a woman outside who refused to give him her car. He was arrested shortly after the shootings.

Xerox killings

■ **HONOLULU, HI**   **11/2/1999**   **BYRAN K. UYESUGI, 40**

Uyesugi, a Xerox service technician, opened fire inside the building with a 9mm Glock. He fled and was later apprehended by police.

Wedgwood Baptist Church shooting

■ **FORT WORTH, TX**   **9/15/1999**   **LARRY G. ASHBROOK, 47**

Ashbrook opened fire inside the Wedgwood Baptist Church during a prayer rally before committing suicide.

Atlanta day-trading spree killings

■ **ATLANTA, GA**   **7/29/1999**   **MARK O. BARTON, 44**

Barton, a day trader who had recently lost a substantial sum of money, went on a shooting spree through two day-trading firms. He started at the All-Tech Investment Group, where he worked, then went on to Momentum Securities. He fled and hours later, after being cornered by police outside a gas station, committed suicide. (Two days before the spree, he killed his wife and two children with a hammer.)

Columbine High School massacre

■ **LITTLETON, CO**   **4/20/1999**   **ERIC HARRIS, 18; DYLAN KLEBOLD, 17**

Harris and Klebold opened fire throughout Columbine High School before committing suicide.

Thurston High School shooting

■ **SPRINGFIELD, OR**   **5/21/1998**   **KIPLAND P. KINKEL, 15**

Kinkel, after he was expelled for having a gun in his locker, a freshman at Thurston High School, went on a shooting spree, killing his parents at home and two students at school. Five classmates wrestled Kinkel to the ground before he was arrested.

Westside Middle School killings

■ **JONESBORO, AR**   **3/24/1998**   **MITCHELL S. JOHNSON, 13; ANDREW D. GOLDEN, 11**

Johnson and Golden, two juveniles, ambushed students and teachers as they left the school; they were apprehended by police at the scene.

Connecticut Lottery shooting

■ **NEWINGTON, CT**   **3/6/1998**   **MATTHEW BECK, 35**

Beck, a lottery worker, gunned down four bosses over a salary dispute before committing suicide.

Caltrans maintenance yard shooting

■ **ORANGE, CA**   **12/18/1997**   **ARTURO R. TORRES, 41**

Torres, a former Caltrans employee, opened fire at a maintenance yard after he was fired for allegedly selling government materials he'd stolen from work. He was shot dead by police.

R.E. Phelon Company shooting

■ **AIKEN, SC**   **9/15/1997**   **ARTHUR WISE, 43**

Wise, an ex-con, opened fire at the R. E. Phelon Company in retaliation for being fired after an argument with a supervisor. He attempted suicide by ingesting insecticide, failed, and was executed by the state of South Carolina eight years later.

Fort Lauderdale revenge shooting

■ **FORT LAUDERDALE, FL**   **2/9/1996**   **CLIFTON MCCREE, 41**

McCree, a fired city park employee, opened fire on former coworkers he called "racist devils" inside their municipal trailer in an act of revenge after failing a drug test. He then committed suicide.

Walter Rossler Company massacre

■ **CORPUS CHRISTI, TX**   4/3/1995   **JAMES D. SIMPSON, 28**

Simpson, a disgruntled former metallurgist, opened fire throughout the Walter Rossler Company where he had worked before exiting the building and committing suicide.

Air Force base shooting

■ **FAIRCHILD AIR FORCE BASE, WA**   6/20/1994   **DEAN A. MELLBERG, 20**

Mellberg, a former airman, opened fire inside a hospital at the Fairchild Air Force Base before he was shot dead by a military police officer outside.

Chuck E. Cheese's killings

■ **AURORA, CO**   12/14/1993   **NATHAN DUNLAP, 19**

Dunlap, a recently fired Chuck E. Cheese's employee, went on a rampage through his former workplace and was arrested the following day.

Long Island Rail Road massacre

■ **GARDEN CITY, NY**   12/7/1993   **COLIN FERGUSON, 35**

Ferguson opened fire on an eastbound Long Island Rail Road train as it approached a Garden City station. He was later arrested.

Luigi's shooting

■ **FAYETTEVILLE, NC**   8/6/1993   **KENNETH J. FRENCH, 22**

French, an army sergeant, opened fire inside Luigi's Italian restaurant while ranting about gays in the military before he was shot and arrested by police.

101 California Street shootings

■ **SAN FRANCISCO, CA**   7/1/1993   **GIAN L. FERRI, 55**

Ferri, a failed businessman, opened fire throughout an office building before he committed suicide inside as police pursued him.

Watkins Glen killings

■ **WATKINS GLEN, NY**   10/15/1992   **JOHN T. MILLER, 50**

Miller killed four child-support workers in a county office building before turning the gun on himself. Miller was upset about a court order garnishing his paycheck to cover overdue child-support payments.

Lindhurst High School shooting
■ **OLIVEHURST, CA**   **5/1/1992**   **ERIC HOUSTON, 20**

Houston, a former Lindhurst High School student, angry about various personal failings, killed three students and a teacher at the school before surrendering to police after an eight-hour standoff. He was later sentenced to death.

Royal Oak postal shootings
■ **ROYAL OAK, MI**   **11/14/1991**   **THOMAS MCILVANE, 31**

McIlvane, a laid-off postal worker, opened fire at his former workplace before committing suicide.

University of Iowa shooting
■ **IOWA CITY, IA**   **11/1/1991**   **GANG LU, 28**

Lu, a former graduate student, went on a rampage on campus and then committed suicide at the scene.

Luby's massacre
■ **KILLEEN, TX**   **10/16/1991**   **GEORGE H. HENNARD, 35**

Hennard drove his pickup truck into a Luby's Cafeteria and opened fire before committing suicide.

GMAC massacre
■ **JACKSONVILLE, FL**   **6/18/1990**   **JAMES E. POUGH, 42**

Pough opened fire at a General Motors Acceptance Corporation office before committing suicide. (The day prior, Pough killed a pimp and prostitute and injured two others. Those victims are not included in the mass murder count.)

Standard Gravure shooting
■ **LOUISVILLE, KY**   **9/14/1989**   **JOSEPH T. WESBECKER, 47**

Wesbecker gunned down eight people at his former workplace before committing suicide.

Stockton schoolyard shooting
■ **STOCKTON, CA**   **1/17/1989**   **PATRICK PURDY, 26**

Purdy, an alcoholic with a police record, launched an assault at Cleveland Elementary School, where many young Southeast Asian immigrants were enrolled. Purdy killed himself with a shot to the head.

ESL shooting

■ **SUNNYVALE, CA**   **2/16/1988**   **RICHARD FARLEY, 39**

Farley, a former ESL Incorporated employee, gunned down seven people at his former workplace. He was later arrested and now sits on death row at San Quentin.

Shopping centers spree killings

■ **PALM BAY, FL**   **4/23/1987**   **WILLIAM CRUSE, 59**

Cruse, a retired librarian, was paranoid neighbors gossiped that he was gay. He drove to a Publix supermarket, killing two Florida Tech students en route before opening fire outside and killing a woman. He then drove to a Winn-Dixie supermarket and killed three more, including two police officers. Cruse was arrested after taking a hostage and died on death row in 2009.

United States Postal Service shooting

■ **EDMOND, OK**   **8/20/1986**   **PATRICK SHERRILL, 44**

Sherrill, a postal worker, opened fire at a post office before committing suicide.

San Ysidro McDonald's massacre

■ **SAN YSIDRO, CA**   **7/18/1984**   **JAMES O. HUBERTY, 41**

Huberty opened fire in a McDonald's restaurant before he was shot dead by a police officer.

Dallas nightclub shooting

■ **DALLAS, TX**   **6/29/1984**   **ABDELKRIM BELACHHEB, 39**

Belachheb opened fire at an upscale nightclub after a woman rejected his advances. He was later arrested.

Welding shop shooting

■ **MIAMI, FL**   **8/20/1982**   **CARL R. BROWN, 51**

Brown, a junior high school teacher, opened fire inside a welding shop and was later shot dead by a witness as he fled the scene.

American Indian Tribes with Some Level of Established Wellness Courts

T he prevalence of healing and wellness programs operating in tribal courts among American Indian tribes is remarkable, notable, and encouraging. This list includes tribes that are now operating or recently operated therapeutic or healing programs within the court system. I am certain the list will continue to expand, and encourage anyone in need of the kind of services offered to use the list as a resource.

Alabama
Poarch Band of Creek Indians
   Poarch Band of Creek Indians Adult Drug Court

Alaska
Kenaitze Indian Tribe
   Kenaitze Juvenile Healing to Wellness Court
Native Village of Barrow
   Native Village of Barrow Juvenile Wellness Court

Arizona
Colorado River Indian Tribes
    Colorado River Healing to Wellness Court
Fort McDowell Yavapai Nation
    Fort McDowell Adult & Juvenile Healing to Wellness Court
Gila River Indian Community
    Gila River Indian Community Court—Juvenile Drug Court
    Gila River Juvenile Healing to Wellness Court
Hopi Tribe
    Hopi Juvenile Healing to Wellness Court
Kaibab Band of Paiute Indians
    Kaibab-Paiute Adult Healing to Wellness Court
Pascua Yaqui Tribe
    Pascua Yaqui Adult Healing to Wellness Court
Salt River Pima-Maricopa Indian Community
    Salt River Juvenile Healing to Wellness Court
San Carlos Apache-Ndeh Nation
    San Carlos Adult & DWI Healing to Wellness Court
Tonto Apache Tribe
    Tonto Apache Healing to Wellness Court
White Mountain Apache
    White Mountain Apache Healing to Wellness Court
Yavapai-Apache Nation
    Yavapai-Apache Adult Healing to Wellness Court

California
Hoopa Valley Tribe
    Hoopa Valley Juvenile Healing to Wellness Court
Karuk Tribe
    Karuk Juvenile Healing to Wellness Court
La Jolla Band of Luiseno Indians
    La Jolla Healing to Wellness Court
Yurok Tribe
    Yurok Adult Healing to Wellness Court

Colorado
Southern Ute Indian Tribe
> Southern Ute tüüÇai (Wellness) Court

Idaho
Coeur d'Alene Tribe
> Coeur d'Alene Adult Healing to Wellness Court

Nez Perce Tribe of Idaho
> Nez Perce Adult Healing to Wellness Court

Iowa
Sac & Fox Tribe of the Mississippi in Iowa/Meskwaki Nation
> Sac & Fox Adult & Family Healing to Wellness Court (no longer in operation)

Kansas
Kickapoo Tribe of Indians
> Kickapoo Adult Healing to Wellness Court

Prairie Band of Potawatomie Nation
> Prairie Band Adult Healing to Wellness Court

Maine
Penobscot Indian Nation
> Penobscot Adult & Juvenile Healing to Wellness Court

Michigan
Bay Mills Indian Community
> Bay Mills Adult Healing to Wellness Court

Grand Traverse Band of Ottawa & Chippewa Indians
> Odeswaning Inama Mikana Grand Traverse Band Healing to Wellness Drug Court

Keweenaw Bay Indian Community
> Keweenaw Bay Adult Healing to Wellness Court

Little Traverse Bay Bands of Odawa Indians
> Waabshki-Miigwan (White Feather) Program

Sault Ste. Marie Tribe of Chippewa Indians
> Sault Ste. Marie Adult Healing to Wellness Court

Minnesota
Leech Lake Band of Ojibwe Indians
> Leech Lake–Cass County–Itasca County DWI/Adult Healing to Wellness Court (Joint Tribal-State Jurisdiction)

Red Lake Band of Chippewa Indians
> Red Lake Adult, Juvenile, & Family Wellness Court

White Earth Nation
> White Earth Juvenile Healing to Wellness Court
> White Earth Nation & Mahnomen County DWI Court

Mississippi
Mississippi Band of Choctaw Indians
> Mississippi Choctaw Adult & Juvenile Healing to Wellness Courts

Montana
Blackfeet Nation
> Blackfeet Tribal Wellness Court (not currently operational)

Chippewa Cree Tribe of the Rocky Boy's Reservation of Montana
> Chippewa Cree Adult Healing to Wellness Court

Crow Tribe
> Crow Tribe Apsaalooke Juvenile Wellness Court

Fort Peck Assiniboine & Sioux Tribes
> Fort Peck DUI & Family Healing to Wellness Courts

Nebraska
Omaha Tribe of Nebraska
> Omaha DWI Healing to Wellness Court

Winnebago Tribe of Nebraska
> Winnebago Juvenile Healing to Wellness Court

Nevada
Fallon Paiute Shoshone Tribe
> Central Nevada Regional Tribal Wellness Court

Reno-Sparks Indian Colony
> Reno-Sparks Adult & DWI Healing to Wellness Court

Shoshone-Paiute Tribes of the Duck Valley Indian Reservation
    Shoshone-Paiute Drug Court

New Mexico
Mescalero Apache Tribe
    Mescalero Apache Adult Healing to Wellness Court
Navajo Nation
    Alamo-To'hajiilee Judicial District
    Alamo-To'hajiilee Treatment Court
Pueblo of Acoma
    Acoma Pueblo Adult Healing to Wellness Court
Pueblo of Laguna
    Laguna Pueblo Adult Healing to Wellness Court
    Pueblo of Laguna–Community Wellness Court
Pueblo of Pojoaque
    Pojoaque Healing to Wellness Court
Pueblo of Sandia
    Sandia Pueblo Adult, Juvenile, & Family Healing to Wellness Courts
Pueblo of Zia
    Zia Pueblo Adult & Juvenile Healing to Wellness Court
Pueblo of Zuni
    Zuni Pueblo Healing to Wellness Court

New York
Saint Regis Mohawk Tribe
    Saint Regis Mohawk Healing to Wellness/Drug Court

North Carolina
Eastern Band of Cherokee Indians
    Eastern Band of Cherokee Adult & Juvenile Healing to Wellness Courts

North Dakota
Spirit Lake Tribe
    Spirit Lake Adult, Juvenile, Family, & DWI Court
Three Affiliated Tribes: Mandan, Hidatsa, & Arikara Nations
    Family Fort Berthold Healing to Wellness Court Program

Turtle Mountain Band of Chippewa Indians
　　Turtle Mountain Adult Healing to Wellness Court (not currently operational)

Oklahoma
Cherokee Nation
　　Juvenile Healing to Wellness Court
Cheyenne & Arapaho Tribes
　　Cheyenne & Arapaho Healing to Wellness Court
Citizen Potawatomi Nation
　　Citizen Potawatomi Adult Healing to Wellness Court
Muscogee Creek Nation
　　Muscogee Creek Family Drug Court (no longer operational)

South Dakota
Lower Brule Sioux Tribe
　　Lower Brule Adult Healing to Wellness Court
Rosebud Sioux Tribe of the Sicanqu Oyate
　　Rosebud Sioux Juvenile & Family Healing to Wellness Court
Sisseton-Wahpeton Oyate of the Lake Traverse Indian Reservation
　　Sisseton-Wahpeton Oyate Adult & DWI Healing to Wellness Court

Texas
Ysleta del Sur Pueblo
　　Na Peuykam Chibel (Juvenile) Court

Washington
Chehalis Tribe
　　Juvenile Healing to Wellness Court
Confederated Tribes & Bands of Yakama Nation
　　Yakama Nation Healing to Wellness Drug Court
Lower Elwha Klallam Tribe
　　Strong Peoples Healing Court
Lummi Nation
　　Lummi Adult Healing to Wellness Court
Makah Tribe
　　Makah Adult Healing to Wellness Court

Quileute Nation
> Quileute Healing to Wellness Court

Quinault Indian Nation
> Quinault Adult & Juvenile Wellness Court

Snoqualmie Tribe
> Snoqualmie Juvenile & Family Healing to Wellness Court (no longer operational)

Spokane Tribe
> Spokane Tribal Drug Court

Suquamish Tribe
> Suquamish Adult Wellness Court

Swinomish Indian Tribal Community
> Swinomish Adult Healing to Wellness Court

Wisconsin

Ho-Chunk Nation
> Ho-Chunk Adult Healing to Wellness Court
> Ho-Chunk Family Healing to Wellness Court
> Wa Ehi Hoci Court

Lac du Flambeau Band of Lake Superior Chippewa
> Zaagiibagaa Healing to Wellness Court
> Lac du Flambeau Juvenile Drug Court

Menominee Indian Tribe
> Menipeniw Adult Wellness Court

Wyoming

Eastern Shoshone Tribe & Northern Arapaho Tribe of the Wind River Indian Reservation
> Shoshone & Arapaho Adult Substance Abuse Court
> Shoshone & Araphao Juvenile Substance Abuse Court
> Shoshone & Arapaho Tribal Wellness Court

Source: Tribal Healing To Wellness Courts, Tribal Law and Policy Institute, http://www.wellnesscourts.org/state.cfm?topic=54.

NOTES

PREFACE

1. The subject of this book is mass murders and violence. It contains material that is disturbing to read and might be triggering to survivors of violence.

2. *State v. St. Louis*, 128 Conn. App.703 (Conn App 2011) cert. denied, 302 Conn. 945, 30 A.3d 1 (2011) and *State v. St. Louis,* 146 Conn. App. 461 (Conn App 2013). I testified as an expert witness in the habeas corpus trial of convicted murderer Chadwick St. Louis. St. Louis was convicted of murdering a friend, burying his body at a work site, and lying to St. Louis's family about the heinous crime.

3. Richard E. Redding, *Why It Is Essential to Teach about Mental Health Issues in Criminal Law*, 14 Wash. U. Journal and Pol'y 407, 410 (2004).

4. Kenneth R. Feinberg, Who Gets What: Fair Compensation after Tragedy and Financial Upheaval (2012).

CHAPTER ONE. COUNTING VICTIMS: AN INTRODUCTION TO INDIGENOUS VS. NON-INDIGENOUS PERSPECTIVES

1. Hunter Stuart, *Sandy Hook Hoax Theories Explained: Why Newtown "Truther" Arguments Don't Hold Up*, Huffington Post (February 11, 2013).

2. Kevin Sullivan, *In Newtown, Nancy Lanza a Subject of Sympathy for Some, Anger for Others*, Washington Post (December 19, 2012).

3. Alaine Griffin and Josh Kovner, *Memorial Service Held for Nancy Lanza*, Hartford Courant (June 1, 2013).

4. Stephen J. Sedensky III, *Report of the State's Attorney for the Judicial District of Danbury on the Shootings at Sandy Hook Elementary School and 36 Yogananda Street, Newtown, Connecticut on December 14, 2012* (November 25, 2013).

5. *Id.*

6. Carol Kuruvilla and Vera Chinese, *Families of Newtown Victims Say Adam Lanza's Mom Shares Blame for Raising a Murderer*, New York Daily News (November 28, 2013).

7. Andrew Solomon, *The Reckoning: The Father of the Sandy Hook Killer Searches for Answers*, New Yorker (March 7, 2014), 2.

8. E-mail from Alissa Parker to the author, September 23, 2016.

9. Solomon, *The Reckoning*, 13. *See also* Shushanna Walsh, *The Location of Adam Lanza's Body, Like Most Mass Shooters, Is Unknown*, ABC News, Good Morning America (December 31, 2012).

10. Harold J. Berman, Law and Revolution: The Formation of the Western Legal Tradition, 183 (1983).

11. Robert Yazzie, *Life Comes of It*, in Navajo Nation Peacemaking, 44 (Marianne O. Nielson and James W. Zion eds., 2005).

12. Yazzie, *Life Comes of It*, 46.

13. Juan Tauri and Allison Morris, *Reforming Justice: The Potential of Maori Processes*, 30 Australian and New Zealand Journal of Criminology, 149, 150 (1997). Tauri and Morris loosely translate *runanga o nga tura* as a council or a court.

14. Yazzie, *Life Comes of It*, 46.

15. *See* Yazzie, *Life Comes of It*, 46. For information on the peacemaking program, *see* The Peacemaking Program of the Navajo Nation, http://www.navajocourts.org/indexpeacemaking.htm.

CHAPTER TWO. RAMPAGE MURDERS: SCHOOL SHOOTINGS IN NON-INDIGENOUS COMMUNITIES

1. *See* Ben "Ziggy" Williamson, *The Gunslinger to the Ivory Tower Came: Should Universities Have a Duty to Prevent Rampage Killings?* Fla. L. Rev. 895, 895 & n.1 (2008). Many terms are used in academic references to describe the same type of occurrence. *See also* James Alan Fox and Jack Levin, *Multiple Homicide: Patterns of Serial and Mass Murder*, 23 Crime & Just. 407, 408, 437 (1998) (mass murder, spree killing, going berserk, running amok), and Helen Hickey de Haven, *The Elephant in the Ivory Tower: Rampages in Higher Education and the Case for Institutional Liability*, 35 J.C. & U.L. 503 (2009).

2. Katherine S. Newman et al., Rampage: The Social Roots of School Shootings, 15 (2004).

3. Ronald M. Holmes and Stephen T. Holmes, *Understanding Mass Murder: A Starting Point*, 56 Fed. Probation 53 (1992). *See* James Alan Fox et al., The Will to Kill: Making Sense of Senseless Murder 408, 437 (2012).

4. Holmes and Holmes, *Understanding Mass Murder*, 53.

5. Ronald M. Holmes and J. Deberger, *Profiles in Terror: The Serial Murderer*, 49(3) Fed. Probation 29–34 (1988). R. Hazelwood and J. Douglas, *The Lust Murder*, 49(4) FBI Law Enforcement Bulletin 1–8 (1980).

6. The focus of my study is on mass shootings in the United States, although they occur throughout the world.

7. Newman et al., Rampage, 14.

8. Dave Cullen, Columbine, 32 (2009).

9. *Id.* at 359.

10. *Id.* at 32. According to Cullen, Eric Harris bragged in his journal about killing more people than McVeigh killed.

11. *Id.*

12. *Id.*

13. *Id.*

14. *Id.* at 33.

15. *Id.* at 44.

16. Gina Lamb, *Times Topics, Columbine High School*, New York Times (updated April 17, 2008).

17. *Id.*

18. Cullen, Columbine, 67.

19. *Id.* at 353.

20. *Id.* at 102.

21. *Columbine High School Shootings Fast Facts*, CNN.com.

22. Lamb, *Times Topics.*

23. Susan Donaldson James, ABC News (April 13, 2009).

24. Glenn W. Muschert, *Media and Massacre: The Social Construction of the Columbine Story*, Doctoral Dissertation, University of Colorado at Boulder, 2002, 96–97, as cited in Glenn W. Muschert, *Frame-changing in the Media Coverage of a School Shooting: The Rise of Columbine as a National Concern*, 46 Social Science Journal 165 (2009).

25. *Id.* at 165.

26. *Id.*

27. *Stoddart v. Pocatello School Dist. #25*, 239 P.3d 784 (2010).

28. *Shooter: You Have Blood on Your Hands*, CNN.com (April 18, 2007).

29. Stephen J. Sedensky III, *Report of the State's Attorney for the Judicial District of Danbury on the Shootings at Sandy Hook Elementary School and 36 Yogananda Street, Newtown, Connecticut on December 14, 2012* (November 25, 2013), 3.

30. Pat Pheifer, *Waseca Teen Accused in School Shooting Plot Had Been Planning for Months*, Star Tribune (May 2, 2014).

31. The actual name of this school is Virginia Polytechnic Institute and State University.

32. Virginia Tech, https://www.vt.edu/.

33. Report of the Review Panel, *Mass Shootings at Virginia Tech*, 21 (August 2007).

34. *Id.* at 24.

35. *Id.* at 26.

36. *Id.* at 25.

37. Chris Herring, *Report Faults Virginia Tech in Shootings*, Wall Street Journal (December 5, 2009).

38. Thane Burnett, *Virginia Tech Massacre, Cho, Hilscher Had No Link*, London Free Press (April 19, 2007).

39. Report of the Review Panel, 27.

40. *Id.* at 91.

41. *Id.* at 27.

42. Matti Friedman, *Holocaust Survivor Killed in VA Shooting*, Washington Post (April 17, 2007).

43. Report of the Review Panel, 28.

44. *Id.* at 92.

45. Sedensky, *Report of the State's Attorney*, 5. Edmund H. Mahoney and Dave Altimari, *A Methodical Massacre: Horror and Heroics*, Hartford Courant (December 15, 2012).

46. Sedensky, *Report of the State's Attorney*, 22.

47. Mahoney and Altimari, *A Methodical Massacre*.

48. Sedensky, *Report of the State's Attorney*, 10.

49. Mahoney and Altimari, *A Methodical Massacre*.

50. Sedensky, *Report of the State's Attorney*, 10.

51. *Id.*

52. Peter Applebome and Michael Wilson, *Who Would Do This to Our Poor Little Babies*, New York Times (December 14, 2012).

53. James Barron, *Children Were All Shot Multiple Times*, New York Times (December 15, 2012).

54. Two of the children died at Danbury Hospital.

55. Applebome and Wilson, *Who Would Do This to Our Poor Little Babies.*

CHAPTER THREE. WHEN MASS SHOOTINGS OCCUR ON AMERICAN INDIAN RESERVATIONS: STUDIES IN CONTRAST

1. Tina Norris, Paula L. Vines and Elizabeth M. Hoeffel, *The American Indian and Alaska Native Population: 2010*, (2012), https://www.census.gov/history/pdf/c2010br-10.pdf.

2. United States Census, American FactFinder, https://factfinder.census.gov/faces/nav/jsf/pages/index.xhtml.

3. Indian Affairs Council, State of Minnesota, http://mn.gov/indianaffairs/tribes_redlake.html.

4. *Id.*

5. *Id.*; Indian General Allotment Act, February 8, 1887, c.119, 24 Stat. 390.

6. Indian Affairs Council, fn 1.

7. Red Lake Tribal History, Official Site of the Red Lake Nation, http://www.redlakenation.org/index.asp?SEC=C4DEC6ED-B3F1–4CFA-95A3–9260D0073AA0&Type=B_BASIC.

8. Indian Affairs Council.

9. Mary Ellen O'Toole, *Jeffrey Weise and the Shooting at Red Lake Minnesota High School: A Behavioral Perspective*, in School Shootings 178 (Nils Bockler et al., eds., 2013).

10. *Id.*

11. O'Toole, *Jeffrey Weise and the Shooting at Red Lake*, 130. The ownership and source of this gun remains unknown to this day.

12. *Id.*

13. O'Toole, *Jeffrey Weise and the Shooting at Red Lake*, 181.

14. John Rosengren, *Everyday Hero: Jeff May*, Reader's Digest (September, 2005).

15. *Id.*

16. O'Toole, *Jeffrey Weise and the Shooting at Red Lake*, 181.

17. *Id.*

18. *Id.*

19. Boyd Huppert, *Red Lake School Shooting Survivor Shares Her Story*, Kare 11 News (May 2, 2010), http://www.kare11.com/news/article/849250/0/Red-Lake-School-shooting-survivor-shares-her-story.

20. Rosengren, *Everyday Hero.*

21. *Id. See also* Howie Padilla, *A Long Year at Red Lake: Suddenly It Was Up to Shane*, Star Tribune (March 19, 2006).

22. O'Toole, *Jeffrey Weise and the Shooting at Red Lake*, 181.

23. *Id.* at 182.

24. Reports differ as to whether the tribal police wounded Weise.

25. Padilla, *A Long Year at Red Lake*.

26. *Grief and Shock after Red Lake School Shootings*, Indian Country Today (March 30, 2005).

27. Dana Hedgpeth, *Tribe Responds to Killings with Grief Rather Than Anger*, Washington Post (March 27, 2005).

28. *Id.*

29. *Id.*

30. *Id.*

31. Padilla, *A Long Year at Red Lake*.

32. *Id.*

33. P. J. Huffstutter, *Red Lake Reservation Readies Burial Rituals*, Los Angeles Times (March 24, 2005).

34. *Id.*

35. *Three Red Lake Shooting Victims Buried*, Washington Times (March 27, 2005).

36. *Id.*

37. *Id.*

38. *What Happened at Red Lake on March 21, 2005?* Red Lake Nation News (March 21, 2012).

39. *Id.*

40. Hedgpeth, *Tribe Responds to Killings*.

41. *Id.*

42. *Tribal Elders Protective of Red Lake Culture*, Minnesota Public Radio (March 25, 2005).

43. Tom Scheck, *Red Lake Buries Four on Monday*, Minnesota Public Radio (March 28, 2005).

44. *Id.*

45. *Id.*

46. R. S. Littlefield et al., *A Case Study of the Red Lake, Minnesota, School Shooting: Intercultural Learning in the Renewal Process*, 2(3) Communication, Culture & Critique 361–383 (2009).

47. *Id.*

48. Littlefield, *Case Study of the Red Lake, Minnesota, School Shooting*, 372. *See also* the article *Red Lake Tribal Council Defends Aid to Shooter's Family*, Rockford Register Star (April 15, 2005). For funds created at Wells Fargo Bank, *see* C. Haga, *Every Piece but "Why,"* Star Tribune (March 23, 2005); for Red Lake funds, *see* R. Franklin, *Red Lake School Shootings: Reservation Families Pull Together*, Star Tribune (March 24, 2005); for funds from the Blandin Foundation, *see* P. Levy, *Red Lake Band Gets Blandin Grant for Youth*, Star Tribune (July 21, 2005); for Minnesota state resources, *see* T. Collins, *School Restart Delayed in Red Lake*, Star Tribune (April 8, 2005).

49. *Red Lake Tribal Council Defends Aid to Shooter's Family*, Rockford Register Star (April 15, 2005).

50. *Tribe Gives Victims Aid to Shooter's Family, Citing a "Double Burden,"* Los Angeles Times (April 15, 2005). *See also* the article *National Briefing Midwest: Minnesota*, New York Times (April 12, 2005).

51. *Tribe Gives Victims Aid to Shooter's Family.*

52. *Id.* Note: The *Los Angeles Times* reports that this quote was first reported by the *St. Paul Pioneer Press.*

53. *Id. See also* T. Robertson, *Tensions within Red Lake Tribe Reach Surface*, Minnesota Public Radio (April 15, 2005).

54. *Tribe Gives Victims Aid to Shooter's Family.* Note: The *Los Angeles Times* reports that this quote was first reported by the *Star Tribune* of Minneapolis.

55. *Id.*

56. *Id.*

57. Austin, Navajo Courts and Common Law, 87.

58. Red Lake Nation, Frequently Asked Questions, http://www.redlakenation.org/index. asp?SEC=B0AF61D3–9004–46BC-891D-EC895B6BFFD6&Type=B_LIST.

59. Elisabeth Wiley, *Sheriff: Wash. Shooter Arranged To Meet His Friends via Text*, USA Today (October 28, 2014), https://perma.cc/7CZN-J82J. See also Kirk Johnson, Ian Lovett, and Michael Paulson, *2 Die, Including Gunman, in Shooting at Washington State High School*, New York Times (October 24, 2014).

60. Wiley, *Sheriff.*

61. *Id.*

62. Associated Press, *Fifth Teen Dies Following Washington School Shooting*, Washington Post (November 8, 2014).

63. *Marysville Shooting Victim to Have Jaw Surgery Thursday*, New York Times (October 30, 2014).

64. Mike Carter, *Father of Marysville Shooter Sentenced to Two Years for Illegal Gun Possession*, Seattle Times (January 11, 2016).

65. Max Kutner, *What Led Jaylen Fryberg to Commit the Deadliest High School Shooting in a Decade?*, Newsweek (September 16, 2015).

66. Richard Walker, *After Wash. State School Tragedy Northwest Communities Focus on Love, Healing and Forgiveness*, Indian Country Today Media Network (November 12, 2014).

67. *Id.*

68. *Id.*

69. Kutner, *What Led Jaylen Fryberg.*

70. *Id.*

71. Public Statement of the Tulalip Tribes, October 29, 2014, http://www.tulaliptribes-nsn. gov/Home.aspx.

72. Scott North, *Tulalip Tribes Quietly Mark the Death of the Marysville Shooter*, Everett Herald (October 30, 2014).

73. *Id.*

74. *California: 4 Killed at Indian Tribal Meeting*, New York Times (February 21, 2014).

75. *Cherie Rhoades Pleads Not Guilty to Murder Charges*, KOBI-TV (November 10, 2014)

76. *People v. Cherie Rhoades*, Case No.: F-14–073 (Cal. Super. Ct.).

77. Jane Braxton Little, *Former Tribal Chair Sentenced to Death for Slaughtering Family Members During Hearing to Evict Her*, Sacramento Bee (January 6, 2017).

78. David Boroff, *Gunman Kills Four Members of Own Family and Wounds Two Others on California Indian Reservation*, New York Daily News (December 10, 2012).

79. Adrian Glass-Moore, *Fatal Shootings in Sisseton Sparked by Domestic Dispute*, Forum of Fargo-Moorhead (December 19, 2014), http://www.inforum.com/news/crime/3638788-fatal-shootings-sisseton-sparked-domestic-dispute.

80. Levi Rickert, *Four Dead from Shooting on Lake Traverse Reservation*, Native News Online, http://nativenewsonline.net/currents/four-dead-shooting-lake-traverse-reservation/.

CHAPTER FOUR. THE TYPICAL AFTERMATH OF RAMPAGE MURDER: THE OUTPOURING OF ANGER AT PARENTS AND FAMILY MEMBERS

1. For example, in connection with the Red Lake rampage, Louis Jourdain, sixteen, was arrested by the Federal Bureau of Investigation and charged with the crime of conspiracy. The teenager is the son of Red Lake Tribal Chairman Floyd Jourdain Jr. *See* Monica Davey and Kirk Johnson, *Tribe Is Shaken by Arrest of Leader's Son in Shootings*, New York Times (March 30, 2005).

2. Susan Klebold, *I Will Never Know Why*, O, the Oprah Magazine (November 2009).

3. *Id.*

4. *Id.*

5. Cullen, Columbine, 278–279 (2009).

6. *Id.* at 278.

7. *Id.*

8. *Id.*

9. Klebold, *I Will Never Know Why.*

10. *Id.*

11. Newman, Rampage, 179.

12. *See* the case *James v. Wilson*, 95 S.W.3d 875, 882 (Ky. Ct. App. 2002).

13. Jenkins, I Choose to Be Happy, 10.

14. *Id.* at 35.

15. *Id.* at 77.

16. *Id.*

17. *Kentucky School Shooter "Guilty but Mentally Ill,"* CNN.com (October 5, 1998).

18. *Id.*; KRS § 504.130. The statute provides: (1) The defendant may be found guilty but mentally ill if: (a) The prosecution proves beyond a reasonable doubt that the defendant is guilty of an offense; and (b) The defendant proves by a preponderance of the evidence that he was mentally ill at the time of the offense; (2) If the defendant waives his right to trial, the court may accept a plea of guilty but mentally ill if it finds that the defendant was mentally ill at the time of the offense.

19. Newman, Rampage, 194.

20. *Kentucky School Shooter "Guilty but Mentally Ill,"* CNN.com.

21. Newman, Rampage, 190–191.

22. *Id.* at 192.

23. *Id.* at 192.

24. *James v. Carneal*, Civ. A. No. 98-CI-01154, Compl., McCracken Cir. Ct., Paducah, Ky. (filed Dec. 2, 1998). Appealed, *James v. Wilson*, 95 S.W.3d 875 (Ky. Ct. App. 2002).

25. Rhonda v. Magee Andrews, *The Justice of Parental Accountability: Hypothetical Disinterested Citizens and Real Victims' Voices in the Debate over Expanded Parental Liability*, 75 Temp. L. Rev. 375, 384 (2002).

26. *Id.* at 385.

27. *Id.*

28. *Id.*

29. *Id.*

30. *Id.*

31. *Id.*

32. Newman, Rampage, 186.

33. *James v. Wilson.*

34. *Id.* at 887.

35. *See e.g.* the suit filed after the Columbine shooting: *Shoels v. Harris*, Case No. 99CV 3518, Compl., Dist. Ct., 2d Jud. Dist., City & County of Denver, Colo. (filed May 27, 1999); the suit filed after the Jonesboro Arkansas shooting: *Wright v. Golden*, CIV 98–394(B), Compl., Cir. Ct., Craighead County, Ark. (filed Aug. 10, 1998); and several suits filed by parents of Sandy Hook, Connecticut, victims, for example, *Mark Mattioli, Co-Administrator of the*

Estate of James Radley Mattioli v. Samuel J. Starks, Administrator of the Estate of Nancy Lanza, Case No. FBT-CV15–6048074-S, Judicial District of Fairfield, CT (filed January 23, 2015). For an account of settlements reached in lawsuits against the estate of Nancy Lanza, *see* Dave Altimari, *Sandy Hook Families Settle Lawsuits against Lanza Estate For $1.5M*, Hartford Courant (August 6, 2015).

36. *See* Jonesboro Compl., at 14–17 (charging gun manufacturer); *see also* the article *Columbine Victims' Families Sue Maker of Anti-Depressant*, Associated Press (October 21, 2001), which reported that plaintiffs had also filed suit against "three men who worked at a gun show where the gunmen got some of their weapons." *See* Paducah Compl., at 83–84 (charging school system, board, administrators, teachers, and employees). See *Shoels v. Stone*, No. 00CV903, Am. Compl. For Damages in Tort, U.S. Dist. Ct., Dist. of Colo. P 20 (filed May 9, 2000) (bringing action against juvenile agencies and officials). *See* Columbine Compl., at 7–19 (charging parents); Paducah Compl., at 77–81 (charging parents). Parents of the victims in Columbine also filed actions against the makers of Luvox, an antidepressant found in therapeutic amounts in Eric Harris' system: *Columbine Victims' Families Sue Maker of Anti-Depressant*. One lawsuit, filed by surviving family members of the Newtown tragedy, have sued Bushmaster, the maker of the gun used by Adam Lanza. That suit is still pending: *Soto v. Bushmaster Firearms LLC*, et al., No. FBT CV-156048103.

37. Jenkins, I Choose to Be Happy, 25.

38. The author testified on behalf of the defense in the habeas corpus case on July 7, 2014, in the Rockville, Connecticut, Superior Court. *See* the case *State of Connecticut v. Chadwick St. Louis*, Docket No. CV10–4003535-S.

39. C.G.S. § 54–85a.

40. *State v. Nguyen* (1999), 52 Conn. App. 85 (Conn. App. 1999), certification granted in part 248 Conn. 913, affirmed, 253 Conn. 639.

41. For the two appeals, *see* the cases *State v. St. Louis*, 128 Conn. App. 703 (Conn. App. 2011) cert. denied, 302 Conn. 945, 30 A. 3d 1 (2011) and *State v. St. Louis*, 146 Conn. App. 461 (Conn. App. 2013); for the petition for sentence review, *see* Connecticut Sentence Review Division, http://jud.ct.gov/SRD_0314.pdf; for the petition for habeas corpus, *see* the case *State of Connecticut v. Chadwick St. Louis*, Docket No. CV10–4003535-S.

42. *State of Connecticut vs. Chadwick St. Louis, Docket No. CR07–0212876-T*, Trial Transcript, March 13, 2009, 8–22.

43. *Id* at 21.

44. *Id* at 24.

45. *Id* at 26.

46. *Id* at 29.

47. *See* chapter 8 for more information on typical law school curriculum. *See also* the case *State v. St. Louis, Docket No. CR07–0212876-T* Trial Transcript, 41.

CHAPTER FIVE. RESTORATIVE JUSTICE IN INDIGENOUS CULTURES: RESTORING BALANCE AND HARMONY

1. *See* Joe Galaway and Burt Hudson, eds., Restorative Justice: International Perspectives, 1 (1996).

2. *See* Michael Barkun, Law without Sanctions: Order in Primitive Societies and the World Community, 1968; Richard Falk, International Jurisdiction: Horizontal and Vertical Conceptions of the Legal Order, Temple L. Q. 32, 295–320 (1959).

3. Kathleen Daly, *Restorative Justice: The Real Story*, 4(55) Punishment & Soc'y 12 (2002).

4. Elmar Weitkamp, *The History of Restorative Justice*, in Restorative Juvenile Justice: Repairing the Harm of Youth Crime, (Gordon Bazemore and Lode Walgrave, eds.,1999).

5. *See* Howard Zehr, Changing Lenses: A New Focus for Crime and Justice, 63 (3d ed. 2005).

6. John Braithwaite, Restorative Justice and Responsive Regulation, 5 (2002).

7. *Id. See also* J. W. Mohr, *Criminal Justice and Christian Responsibility; The Secularization of Criminal Law*, paper presented to the Mennonite Central Committee Canada Annual Meeting, Abbotsford, British Columbia (January 22, 1981).

8. *See e.g.*, Daly, *Restorative Justice*, at fn 102.

9. One example is the Kikuyo of Kenya. After a murder, the victim's family invaded the lands of the murderer. They would call out the family of the murderer by cutting down plants. This invasion was called *king'ore kia muhiriga*. They would kill the murderer or someone from the murderer's family to settle the matter. *See* Sarah Kinyanjui, *Restorative Justice in Traditional Pre-Colonial Criminal Justice Systems in Kenya*, 10 Tribal Law J. 1, 5, http://tlj.unm.edu/volumes/vol10/Kinyanjui.pdf.

10. Jon' A. F. Meyer, *History Repeats Itself: Restorative Justice in Native American Communities*, 14(1) Journal of Contemp. Justice 42, 44 (February 1998).

11. *Id.* at 44.

12. Carrie E. Garrow and Sarah Deer, Tribal Criminal Law and Procedure, 10 (2004).

13. Carole E. Goldberg, *Overextended Borrowing: Tribal Peacemaking Applied in Non-Indian Disputes*, 72 Wash. L. Rev. 1003, 1011 (1997).

14. Peggy v. Beck et al., The Sacred Ways of Knowledge: Sources of Life, 102 (1990).

15. Goldberg, *Overextended Borrowing*, 1011, and at chapter 4, for a discussion of the clan relationships as a distinguishing attribute of the Red Lake Band of Chippewa Indians.

16. Meyer, *History Repeats Itself*, 45.

17. *Id.*

18. *Id.* at 44.

19. *Id.*

20. *Id.*

21. Robert A. Williams Jr., Linking Arms Together, American Indian Treaty Visions of Law and Peace, 1600–1800, 54 (1977).

22. *Id.*

23. *Id.* at 56.

24. Meyer, *History Repeats Itself*, 44.

25. *Id.*

26. *Ex parte Kan-gi-shun-ca* (otherwise known as "Crow Dog"), 3 S. Ct. 396 (1883).

27. Hon. Gaylen L. Box, *Crow Dog: Tribal Sovereignty and Criminal Jurisdiction in Indian Country*, 50 Advoc. 13, 15 (2007).

28. *Id.*

29. *Id. See also* Sidney L. Harring, Crow Dog's Case: American Indian Sovereignty, Tribal Law and United States Law in the Nineteenth Century, 1 (1994).

30. *Id. See also* the case *United States v. Crow Dog*, 3 Dak. 196, 14 NW 437 (1882).

31. *Ex parte Kan-gi-shun-ca.*

32. Patrice H. Kunesh, *Banishment as Cultural Justice in Contemporary Tribal Legal Systems*, 37 N.M. L. Rev. 85, 110 (2007).

33. John O. Omale, *Justice In History: An Examination of "African Restorative Traditions And The Emerging "Restorative Justice: Paradigm*, Volume 2, No. 2, 45, AFR. J. OF CRIMNOLOGY & JUST. STUD., (November 2006).

34. Garrow and Deer, Tribal Criminal Law and Procedure, 26.

35. Austin, Navajo Courts and Navajo Common Law, 53.

36. *Id* at 40.

37. Austin, Navajo Courts and Navajo Common Law, 88.

38. *Office of Navajo Nation President and Vice-President v. Navajo Nation Council*, 9 Am. Tribal Law 46 No. SC-CV-02–10. (Nav. Sup. Ct. May 28, 2010).

39. *In Re Mental Health Services for Bizardi*, 5 Am. Tribal Law 467, 469 (Nav. Sup. Ct. 2004). *See also* the case *Atcitty v. Window Rock District Court*, 7 Nav. R. 227, 230 (Nav. Sup. Ct. 1996).

40. Philmer Bluehouse and James Zion, *Hozhooji Naat'aanii: The Navajo Justice and Harmony Ceremony*, 10.4 Mediation Q. 327 (1993) 331.

41. Clifton Leland Wyman, Navajo Ceremonial System, 536 (1983).

42. *Id.*

43. *Navajo Nation v. Kelly*, 6 Am. Tribal Law 772, 777 (Nav. Sup. Ct. 2006).

44. *Duncan v. Shiprock District Court*, 5 Am. Tribal Law 458, 466 (Nav. Sup. Ct. 2004).

45. *Navajo Common Law II, Navajo Law and Justice*, 9(10) Museum Notes, Museum of Northern Arizona (April 1937).

46. *Id.*

47. *Id.*

48. *Id.*

49. *Id.*

50. *Id.*

51. *Id.*

52. Karl N. Llewellyn and E. Adamson Hoebel, The Cheyenne Way: Conflict and Case Law In Primitive Jurisprudence, vii (1941).

53. *Id.* at 67.

54. *Id.* at 12.

55. *Id.* at 3–6.

56. *Id.* at 133.

57. *Id.*

58. *Id.* at 139.

59. *Id.* at 12.

60. *Id.*

61. *Id.* at 13.

62. *Id.* at 85, referring to the case of Little Wolf who killed Starving Elk, 1879–1880.

63. *Id.* at 9.

CHAPTER SIX. FORGIVENESS: RESTORING SOCIAL BONDS

1. Desmond Tutu, *Without Forgiveness There Is No Future*, in Exploring Forgiveness xiii–xiv (R. D. Enright and J. North, eds., 1998). *See also* Desmond Tutu, No Future without Forgiveness (2000).

2. R. Fehr et al., *The Road to Forgiveness: A Meta-Analytic Synthesis of Its Situational and Dispositional Correlates*, 136 Psychological Bulletin, 894–914, 909 (2010).

3. Friedrich Nietzsche, The Genealogy of Morals: A Polemic (1887).

4. N. G. Wade, W. T. Hoyt, J. E. M. Kidwell, and E. L. Worthington Jr., *Efficacy of Psychotherapeutic Interventions to Promote Forgiveness: A Meta-Analysis*. J. of Consulting & Clinical Psychology (2013). *See also* T. W. Baskin and R. D. Enright, *Intervention Studies on Forgiveness: A Meta-Analysis*, 82 J. of Counseling & Development, 79 (2004); and N. G. Wade, E. L. Worthington Jr., and J. E. Meyer, *But Do They Work? A Meta-Analysis of*

Group Interventions to Promote Forgiveness, in Handbook of Forgiveness, 423–440 (E. L. Worthington Jr., ed., 2005).

5. Wade et al., *Efficacy of Psychotherapeutic Interventions to Promote Forgiveness. See also* N. G. Wade and E. L. Worthington Jr., *Overcoming Unforgiveness: Is Forgiveness the Only Way to Deal with Unforgiveness?*, 81 J. of Counseling & Development, 343–353 (2003).

6. D. E. Davis et al., *Research on Religion/Spirituality and Forgiveness: A Meta-Analytic Review*, Psychology of Religion and Spirituality (2013).

7. Wade and Worthington, *Overcoming Unforgiveness*, at 343–353.

8. Jenkins, I Choose to Be Happy, 64.

9. John Braithwaite, Restorative Justice and Responsive Regulation, 3 (2002).

10. Malcolm David Eckel, A Buddhist Approach to Repentance, in Repentance: A Comparative Perspective, 135 (Amitai Etzioni and David Carney eds., 1997).

11. S. D. Boon and L. M. Sulsky, *Attributions of Blame and Forgiveness in Romantic Relationships: A Policy-Capturing Study*, 12 J. of Personality and Social Psychol., 19–44 (1997). *See also* B. W. Darby and B. R. Schlenker, *Children's Reactions to Apologies*, 43 J. of Personality & Social Psychol., 742–753 (1982).

12. Fehr, *The Road to Forgiveness*.

13. *Id.*

14. D. R. Van Tongeren et al., *Forgiveness and Religion: Update and Current Status*, in Mapping Forgiveness, 53–70 (M. R. Maarmi ed., 2012).

15. M. S. Rye et al., Religious Perspectives on Forgiveness, in Forgiveness: Theory, Research and Practice, 17–40 (M. E. McCullough, K. I. Pargament, and C. E. Thoresen eds., 2000).

16. Berman, Law and Revolution, 166.

17. M. E. McCullough and E. L. Worthington Jr., *Religion and the Forgiving Personality*, 67 J. of Personality 1141–1164 (1999).

18. Eliyahu Touger, Mishneh Torah, chapter 1 (1990).

19. Berman, Law and Revolution, 166.

20. For an overview of the influences of Christian philosophy on Western law, *see* Berman, Law and Revolution, chapter 4, "Theological Sources of the Western Legal Tradition."

21. Berman, Law and Revolution, 179.

22. *Id.*

23. *Id.* at 179, quoting Anselm's Prologion, chapters 9–11.

24. D. E. Davis, J. N. Hook, and E. L. Worthington Jr. *Relational Spirituality and Forgiveness: The Roles of Attachment to God, Religious Coping, and Viewing the Transgression as a Desecration*, 27 J. of Psychol. & Christianity, 293–301 (2008). *See also* P. C. Hill et al., *Conceptualizing Religion and Spirituality: Points of Commonality, Points of Departure*, 30 J.

for the Theory of Social Behav., 51–77 (2000).

25. Davis, Hook and Worthington, *Relational Spirituality.*

26. *Id.*

27. Jeff Benedict, *Witnessing Grief and Compassion in Newtown*, Deseret News (December 18, 2012). According to the Daily News, the funeral of Emilie Parker was held at the Church of Jesus Christ of Latter-day Saints in Ogden, Utah. *See* Chelsea Rose Marcius and Bill Hutchinson, *Tragic Finale: Tears Fall as Last of Newtown's Little Victims Are Laid to Rest*, New York Daily News (December 22, 2012).

28. Jenkins, I Choose to Be Happy, 63.

29. *Id.* at 56–57.

30. Donald Kraybill et al., Amish Grace: How Forgiveness Transcended Tragedy (2010).

31. Donald B. Kraybill, *Forgiving Is Woven into Life of Amish*, Philadelphia Inquirer (October 8, 2006).

32. *Id.*

33. *Id.*

34. Sarah Pulliam Bailey, *The Charleston Shooting Is the Largest Mass Shooting in a House of Worship since 1991*, Washington Post (June 18, 2015).

35. *See* Peggy M. Tobolowsky, *Victim Participation in the Criminal Justice Process: Fifteen Years after the President's Task Force on Victims of Crime*, 25 New Eng. J. on Crim. & Civ. Confinement 21, 32–38, 103–105 (1999).

36. Nikita Stewart and Richard Perez-Pena, *In Charleston, Raw Emotion at Hearing for Suspect in Church Shooting*, New York Times (June 19, 2015).

37. *Id.*

38. Dawn M. Turner, *Emanuel AME Church and the Audacity to Forgive*, Chicago Tribune (September 28, 2015); John S. Dickerson, *Charleston Victims Wield Power*, USA Today (June 21, 2015).

39. Rachel Crosby, *Forgiveness, Reconciliation To Replace Hatred In Charleston*, Las Vegas Review-Journal (April 2, 2018); Bob Smietana, *A Year Later, The Families of Charleston Shooting Victims Still Wrestle With Forgiveness*, Washington Post (June 17, 2016).

40. Barry Paddock and Rich Schapiro, *S.C. Judge Urges Support for Accused Murderer Dylann Roof's Family in Bizarre Court Speech*, New York Daily News (June 19, 2015).

41. Alan Blinder, *Death Penalty Is Sought for Dylann Roof in Charleston Church Killings*, New York Times (May 24, 2016); Alan Binder and Kevin Sack, *Dylann Roof Is Sentenced to Death in Church Massacres*, New York Times (January 10, 2017); Andrew Knapp and Abigail Darlington, *Dylann Roof's 9 Life Sentences on State Murder Charges "Surest" Route to Federal Execution, Prosecutor Says*, Post and Courier (April 10, 2017).

42. Thomas J. Scheff, *Community Conferences: Shame and Anger in Therapeutic Jurisprudence*, 67 Rev. Jur. U.P.R. 97–119 (1999), as reprinted in Judging in a Therapeutic Key, 231–247 (Bruce J. Winick and David B. Wexler, eds., 2003).

43. *Id.*

44. Scheff, *Community Conferences*, 235.

45. Robert D. Carlisle et al., *Do Actions Speak Louder Than Words? Differential Effects of Apology and Restitution on Behavioral and Self-Report Measures of Forgiveness*, 7(4) J. of Positive Psychol. 294–305 (2012).

46. *Id.*

47. A. Lazare, *The Healing Power of Apology*, Family Circle, 12 (September 16, 1997); Aaron Lazare, On Apology (2004).

48. Roy Lavon Brooks, Professor of Law at the University of San Diego School of Law; Brent T. White, *Saving Face: The Benefits of Not Saying I'm Sorry*, 72 Law & Contemp. Probs. 261 (2009).

49. Robert D. Carlisle et al., *Do Actions Speak Louder Than Words*, 294–305 (2012); R. Fehr and M. J. Gelfand, *When Apologies Work: How Matching Apology Components to Victims' Self-Construals Facilitates Forgiveness*, 113 Org. Behav. and Human Decision Processes 37–50 (2010).

50. For more of a discussion about victims and closure, *see* S. Bandes, *When Victims Seek Closure: Forgiveness, Vengeance and the Role of Government*. Fordham Urb. L. J. 27, 1599–1606 (2000). *See also* Antony Pemberton and Sandra Reynaers, *The Controversial Nature of Victim Participation: Therapeutic Benefits in Victim Impact Statements* (January 23, 2011), http://dx.doi.org/10.2139/ssrn.1745923; J. A. Wemmers and E. Erez, Therapeutic Jurisprudence and the Position of Victims (2010).

51. J. A. Wemmers, *Restorative Justice for Victims of Crime: A Victim-oriented Approach to Restorative Justice*, 9 Int'l Rev. of Victimology 43–59 (2002); Ulrich Orth and Andreas Maercker, *Do Trials of Perpetrators Retraumatize Crime Victims?* 19 J. of Interpersonal Violence 2, 212–227 (2004).

52. N. G. Wade et al., *Efficacy of Psychotherapeutic Interventions to Promote Forgiveness: A Meta-Analysis*, J. of Consulting & Clinical Psychology (2013). *See also* Suzanne Freedman, *Forgiveness and Reconciliation: The Importance of Understanding How They Differ*, 42 Counseling and Values (1998).

53. R. D. Enright, Forgiveness Is a Choice: A Step-by-Step Process for Resolving Anger and Restoring Hope (2001); E. L. Worthington Jr., Five Steps to Forgiveness: The Art and Science of Forgiving (2001).

54. Joshua N. Hook et al., *Does Forgiveness Require Interpersonal Interactions? Individual*

Differences in Conceptualization of Forgiveness, 53 Personality & Individual Differences, 687–692 (2012).

55. *Id.*

56. Jeanne Bishop, Change of Heart: Justice, Mercy and Making Peace with My Sister's Killer (2015).

57. *Id.*

58. *Id.* at 111–125.

59. Jenkins, I Choose to Be Happy, 153–162.

60. *Id.* at 212.

61. *Id.* at 219.

62. *Id.* at 220.

63. *Id.*

64. *Id.* at 225.

65. Stephen J. Sedensky III, *Report of the State's Attorney for the Judicial District of Danbury on the Shootings at Sandy Hook Elementary School and 36 Yogananda Street, Newtown, Connecticut on December 14, 2012* (November 25, 2013), http://newtownbee.com/files/Sandy_Hook_Final_Report_1_0.pdf.

66. Sedensky, *Report of the State's Attorney*, 3. The author is a former assistant state's attorney with the Connecticut Division of Criminal Justice (1988–1994), was assigned to the Danbury State's Attorney's Office, and later was a criminal defense attorney regularly handling cases in the Danbury Superior Court, and thus has a professional relationship with Sedensky.

67. Andrew Solomon, *The Reckoning: The Father of the Sandy Hook Killer Searches for Answers*, New Yorker 2 (March 7, 2014).

68. *Id.* at 15.

69. *Id.* at 14–15.

70. *Girl's Parents Meet Father of Gunman in Massacre*, New York Times (March 22, 2013)

71. *Id.*, citing CBS News. *See* http://www.cbsnews.com/news/newtown-victims-parents-do-they-blame-shooters-parents/.

72. E-mail from Alissa Parker to the author, September 23, 2016.

73. *Id.*

74. *Girl's Parents Meet Father of Gunman in Massacre*, New York Times.

75. E-mail from Alissa Parker.

76. *Girl's Parents Meet Father of Gunman in Massacre*.

77. Benedict, *Witnessing Grief and Compassion*.

78. E-mail from Alissa Parker. Madeline is Emilie's younger sister.

79. The statute of limitations in the state of Connecticut for an action brought by an estate for a fatal injury in Connecticut is two years. *See* CGS § 52–55. Although a suit against Peter Lanza was unlikely as Adam Lanza was an adult who lived with his mother, wrongful death tort suits against the estate of Nancy Lanza were possible and in fact were filed. Media reports estimated Nancy Lanza's estate to be valued at $64,000. Ryan Lanza, Peter Lanza's son who was twenty-four at the time of the shootings, is the sole heir of the estate. *See* Dave Altimari, *Nancy Lanza's Will, Which Dates to 1994, Left Estate to Her Sons, Adam and Ryan*, Hartford Courant (April 5, 2013). *See also* Nina Golgowski, *Estate Belonging to Mother of Sandy Hook Shooter, Nancy Lanza Estimated at 64k*, New York Daily News (February 20, 2014).

80. Niraj Chokshi, *Map: There Have Been At Least 74 Shootings at Schools since Newtown,"* Washington Post (June 16, 2014). *See also* appendix 2.

81. Carolyn Mears, Reclaiming School in the Aftermath of Trauma: Advice Based on Experience (2012).

82. Matthew Lysiak, Newtown: An American Tragedy, 251 (2013).

83. *Id.*

84. Ashley Fantz, *Photos Show Shooter's, Victim's Fathers Embracing*, CNN (June 17, 2014), http://www.cnn.com/2014/06/16/justice/california-shooting-fathers-meet-photos/.

85. *Id.*

86. *Id.*

87. Dan Friedman, Joseph Straw, and Corky Siemaszko, *Washington Navy Yard Shooting: Shooter Allowed to Buy Gun Despite Mental Issues, Navy Misconduct*, New York Daily News (September 17, 2013).

88. Eric Badia, Joseph Straw, and Corky Siemaszko, *Mom of Washington Navy Yard Shooter Aaron Alexis Apologizes for Killer As Lawmakers Avoid Action Against NRA*, New York Daily News (September 18, 2013).

89. *Id.*

90. Public Statement of the Tulalip Tribes, October 29, 2014, http://www.tulaliptribes-nsn.gov/Home.aspx.

91. *Id.*

CHAPTER SEVEN. RESTORATIVE JUSTICE AND THERAPEUTIC JURISPRUDENCE TODAY: HOW MUCH CAN BE BORROWED?

1. Bruce J. Winick and David B. Wexler eds., Judging in a Therapeutic Key, 3 (2003).

2. Douglas Sylvester, *Myth in Restorative Justice History*, 2003 Utah L .Rev. 471fn61 (2003). John Braithwaite, *Restorative Justice: Assessing Optimistic and Pessimistic Accounts*, 25

Crime & Just. 1, 2 (1999).

3. Elmar G. M. Weitekamp, *The History of Restorative Justice*, in Restorative Juvenile Justice: Repairing the Harm of Youth Crime, 75 (Gordon Bazemore and Lode Walgrave eds., 1999).

4. *See e.g.*, Kathleen Daly, *Restorative Justice: The Real Story*, 4 Punishment & Soc'y 55 12fn102 (2002).

5. *Id.* at 63.

6. *Id.*

7. *Id.*

8. Sylvester, *Myth in Restorative Justice History*, 501.

9. E. Adamson Hoebel, The Law of Primitive Man (1961).

10. Sylvester, *Myth in Restorative Justice History*, 501.

11. Laura Nader and Elaine Combs-Schilling, *Restitution in Cross-Cultural Perspective*, in Restitution in Criminal Justice, 27 (Burt Galoway and Joe Hudson, eds., 1977); *see also* Sylvester, *Myth in Restorative Justice History* at 501.

12. Robert W. Gordon, *Forward: The Arrival of Critical Historicism*, 49 Stan. L. Rev. 1023, 1023 (1997).

13. Greg Berman and John Feinblatt, *Problem-Solving Courts: A Brief Primer*, in Judging in a Therapeutic Key, 73 (2003).

14. *Id.*

15. Laurie A. Arsenault, *The Great Excavation: "Discovering" Navajo Tribal Peacemaking within the Anglo-American Family System*, 15 Ohio St. J. on Dispute Reso., 795, 800 (199E2000).

16. Leena Kurki, *Incorporating Restorative and Community Justice into American Sentencing and Corrections*, 3 Sent'g Corrections: Issues for the 21st Century (September 1999).

17. West Huddlestine and Douglas Marlowe, *Painting the Current Picture: A National Report on Drug Courts and Other Problem-Solving Court Programs in the United States*, National Drug Court Institute, 37 (2011).

18. Mark Umbreit and Marilyn Peterson Armour, Restorative Justice Dialogue: An Essential Guide for Research and Practice, 1 (2011).

19. *Id.*

20. Mary Ellen Reimund, *Is Restorative Justice on a Collision Course with the Constitution?* 3 Appalachian J. L., 6 (Spring 2004).

21. Mark S. Umbreit, Betty Vos, Robert B. Coates, and Katherine A. Brown, Facing Violence: The Path of Restorative Justice and Dialogue, 115 (2003).

22. *Id.*

23. Umbreit and Peterson Armour, Restorative Justice Dialogue, 112.

24. *Id.* at 118.

25. Frederick W. Gay, Restorative Justice and the Prosecutor, 27 Fordham Urb. L. J. 1651, 1652 (2000).

26. *Id.*

27. Polk County Attorney's Office, VORP, https://www.polkcountyiowa.gov/Attorney/Juvenile/vorp.aspx#facts. Iowa disfavors mediation in cases of domestic violence cases for the same reasons many scholars and professional associations conclude that it is not appropriate: victims of domestic violence face atypical renewed violence, the trauma introduced when victims of domestic violence are in the same room as the offender in mediation sessions, and the difficulty for victims of domestic violence advocating on their own behalf in mediation sessions due to the traumatic nature of domestic violence. For more information, *see: Final Report of The Iowa Supreme Court Mediation and Domestic Violence Work Group* (December 1999).

28. *Id.*

29. Center for Court Innovation, https://www.courtinnovation.org/about.

30. Center for Court Innovation, https://www.courtinnovation.org/areas-of-focus/restorative-justice.

31. Center for Court Innovation, 2016 Annual Report, https://www.courtinnovation.org/sites/default/files/media/documents/2017–10/2016_annual_report.pdf.

32. Jonathan Lippman, *Remarks from the Inaugural Fordham Dispute Resolution Society Symposium: ADR as a Tool for Achieving Social Justice*, 34 Fordham Urb. L. J. 813 (2007). *See also* Lee, C. G. et al., *A Community Court Grows in Brooklyn: A Comprehensive Evaluation of the Red Hook Community Justice Center*, National Center for State Courts (2013), https://www.courtinnovation.org/sites/default/files/media/document/2018/RH_Report.pdf.

33. Sarah Conway, *This Chicago Court Uses Peace Circles to Dole Out Justice*, WBEZ 91.5 Chicago (June 19, 2018), https://www.wbez.org/shows/wbez-news/this-chicago-court-uses-peace-circles-to-dole-out-justice/7bdcf936–6f46–4ae8–999e-23ea460ecd2c.

34. Navajo Nation Judicial Branch, Institutional History of *Hózhǫ́ji Naat'aah*, http://www.navajocourts.org/indexpeaceplanops.htm.

35. Yazzie, *Life Comes of It.*

36. Navajo Nation Judicial Branch.

37. *Id.*

38. *Id.*

39. Navajo Nation Judicial Branch, "*Diné Traditional Peacemaking*," http://www.navajocourts.org/indexpeaceplanops.htm.

40. *Id.*

41. Navajo Nation Judicial Branch, "*Diné Traditional Peacemaking*," http://www.navajocourts. org/indexpeaceplanops.htm.

42. *Id.* at fn 7. *See also* Robert Porter, *Strengthening Tribal Sovereignty through Peacemaking: How the Anglo-American Legal Tradition Destroys Indigenous Societies*, 28 Colum. Hum. Rts. L. Rev. 235, 258–259 (1997).

43. Paulette Running Wolf and Julie A. Rickard, *Talking Circles: A Native American Approach to Experiential Learning*, 31(1) J. of Multicultural Counseling and Development 39–43 (January 2003).

44. Native American Rights Fund (NARF), Frequently Asked Questions about Peacemaking, http://www.narf.org/peacemaking/learn_more/faq.html. *See* Hon. Janine P. Geske and India McCanse, *Neighborhoods Healed through Restorative Justice*, 15 (1) Disp Resol. Mag. 16–18 (Fall 2008). *See also* Running Wolf and Rickard, *Talking Circles*, at fn 318.

45. National Institute of Justice, *Sentencing Circles*, http://nij.gov/topics/courts/restorative-justice/promising-practices/Pages/sentencing-cricles.aspx.

46. Janelle Smith, *Peacemaking Circles: The "Original" Dispute Resolution of Aboriginal People Emerges as the "New" Alternative Dispute Resolution Process*, 24 Hamline J. Pub. L. & Pol'y 329, 346, 323 (2003).

47. NARF, *Peacemaking Tribal Codes and Models*, http://www.narf.org/peacemaking/codes/index.html.

48. Joseph T. Flies-Away and Carrie E. Garrow, *Healing to Wellness Courts: Therapeutic Jurisprudence*, 2013 Mich. St. L. Rev. 403 (2013).

49. *BC Girl Convicted in School Bullying Tragedy*, CBC News (March 26, 2002), http://www.cbc.ca/news/canada/b-c-girl-convicted-in-school-bullying-tragedy-1.308111.

50. Daniel Girard, *Teen Bully Finds Justice, Healing and the Courage to Apologize: Sentencing Circle Requested by Mother of Suicide Victim*, in Judging in a Therapeutic Key, 46 (2003).

51. Ian Bailey, *Dead Girl's Mother Hugs Bullying BC Teenager*, National Post.

52. Girard, *Teen Bully Finds Justice*, 46.

53. *Id.*

54. *Id.* at 45.

55. *Id.* at 46.

56. *Id.*

57. *Id.*

58. John Pratt, *Colonization Power and Silence: A History of Indigenous Justice in New Zealand Society*, in Restorative Justice: International Perspectives, 148 (Burt Galaway and Joe Hudson, eds., 1996). According to Pratt, in 1872 Maori were 2.3 percent of all prisoners

received, but by 1995, this number surged to nearly 50 percent.

59. *Id.*at 151.

60. *Id.* at 148.

61. Scheff, *Community Conferencing.*

62. Gay, Restorative Justice.

63. Benedict, *Witnessing Grief and Compassion.*

64. Goldberg, Overextended Borrowing, 1011.

65. *Id. See also* Robert V. Wolf, *Widening the Circle: Can Peacemaking Work outside of Tribal Communities? A Guide for Planning,* Center for Court Innovation, http://www.courtinnovation.org/sites/default/files/documents/PeacemakingPlanning_2012.pdf.

66. Angela R. Riley, *Good (Native) Governance,* 107 Colum. L. Rev. 1049 (2007).

67. *Id.*

68. Stephen Cornell and Joseph P. Kalt, *Two Approaches to Economic Development on American Indian Reservations: One Works, the Other Doesn't* 7, 12, 16, Joint Occasional Papers on Native Affairs, Paper No. 2005–02 (2006), http://www.nni.arizona.edu/resources/inpp/2005–02_jopna__Two_Approaches.pdf.

69. U.S. Const. Amend. 1. The clause of the amendment states, in the relevant part: "Congress shall make no law respecting an establishment of religion."

CHAPTER EIGHT. A TIME TO HEAL: RECOMMENDATIONS FOR A WAY FORWARD

1. U.S. Const. Amend. V. The amendment states: "No person . . . shall be compelled in a criminal case to be a witness against himself"; *Kastigar v. United States,* 408 U.S. 441, 442 (1972).

2. *Constitutional Requirements—Procedural Due Process, Judicial Review of Administrative Action,* 32 Fed Prac. & Proc. Judicial Review § 8126 (1st edition)(updated April 2014). *See also* Ronald D. Rotunda and John E. Nowak, Treatise on Constitutional Law Substance and Procedure, section 17.2 (3d ed. 1999).

3. *Mitchell v. United States,* 526 U.S. 314 (1999).

4. *Id.*

5. Laura J. Moriarty, *Victim Participation at Parole Hearings: Balancing Victim Offender and Public Interest,* 4 Criminology and Public Pol'y 385, 399 (2005).

6. The importance of punishment and the retributive model of criminal justice increases with the severity of the crime. *See* D. M. Gromet and J. M. Darley, *Restoration and Retribution: How Including Retributive Components Affects the Acceptability of Restorative Justice Procedures,* 19(4), Social Justice Research 395–432 (2006). *See also* A. Pemberton and S. Reynaers, *The Controversial Nature of Victim Participation: Therapeutic Benefits*

in Victim Impact Statements, in Therapeutic Jurisprudence and Victim Participation in Justice: International Perspectives, 229–248 (E. Erez, M. Kilchlinh, & J. J. M. Wemmers, eds., 2011).

7. *United States v. Romero*, 249 F.2d 371(2nd Cir. 1957); 8 Wigmore, Evidence (3d ed. 1940), s 2279; cf. *Brown v. Walker*, 161 U.S. 591, 597–600, 1896.

8. *United States v. Duchi*, 944 F.2d 391, 392 (8th Cir.1991).

9. Federal Sentencing Guidelines, 18 U.S.C s 5k1.1, Substantial Assistance to Authorities, Policy Statement: Upon motion of the government stating that the defendant has provided substantial assistance in the investigation or prosecution of another person who has committed an offense, the court may depart from the guidelines. (a) The appropriate reduction shall be determined by the court for reasons stated that may include, but are not limited to, consideration of the following: (1) the court's evaluation of the significance and usefulness of the defendant's assistance, taking into consideration the government's evaluation of the assistance rendered; (2) the truthfulness, completeness, and reliability of any information or testimony provided by the defendant; and (3) the nature and extent of the defendant's assistance.

10. *James v. Wilson*, 95 S.W.3d 875 (Ky. Ct. App. 2002).

11. Manda Barger, *Heath 20 Years Later*, WPSD Local 6 (November 28, 2017), https://www.wpsdlocal6.com/2017/11/28/20-years-later-michael-carneal/.

12. *School Shooter Michael Carneal Recalls Delusions*, WDRB.com (October 6, 2010), http://www.wdrb.com/story/13279449/school-shooter-michael-carneal-discusses-delusions.

13. Fernanda Santos, *Gunman in Giffords Shooting Sentenced to 7 Life Terms*, New York Times (November 8, 2012).

14. *Arizona Congresswoman Giffords Shot; Doctors "Optimistic" about Recovery Chances*, Arizona Republic (January 8, 2011).

15. Santos, *Gunman in Giffords Shooting*.

16. *Id.*

17. *Id.*

18. Under most victim compensation statutes, a victim of violent crime may be compensated for pecuniary losses. *See In Re Application of Drake*, 47 Ill. Ct. Cl. 563 (Ill. Ct. Cl. 1993). Recovery under a state fund is limited to those crime victims who can prove that they have suffered actual out-of-pocket loss for which they will not be compensated from any other source.

19. Merriam-Webster Dictionary, http://www.merriam-webster.com/dictionary/victim.

20. Brigid Coleman, *Lawyers Who Are Also Social Workers: How to Effectively Combine Two Different Disciplines to Better Serve Clients*, 7 Wash. J. L. & Pol'y 131, 139 (2001). *See also*

Paula Galowitz, *Collaboration between Lawyers and Social Workers: Re-Examining the Nature and Potential of the Relationship*, 67 Fordham L. Rev. 2123 (1999).

21. *Id.*

22. Richard E. Redding, *Why It Is Essential to Teach about Mental Health Issues in Criminal Law*, 14 Wash. U. J. L & Pol'y 425–427 (2004).

23. *Id.*

24. Professor Redding offers a proposed syllabus for the law school course, Criminal Law and Psychology, in his article noted above, *Why It Is Essential to Teach about Mental Health* at 407, 410.

CONCLUSION

1. Final Report of the Sandy Hook Advisory Commission (March 6, 2015), http://www.shac.ct.gov/SHAC_Final_Report_3–6-2015.pdf.

2. Sadly, it appears Richman committed suicide on March 25, 2019. *See,* Michael Gold and Tyler Pager, *Sandy Hook Victim's Father Dies in Apparent Suicide in Newtown*, New York Times (March 25, 2019).

APPENDIX ONE. FATAL VICTIMS IN SELECT MASS SHOOTINGS

1. *Columbine High School Shootings Fast Facts*, CNN.com, http://www.cnn.com/2013/09/18/us/columbine-high-school-shootings-fast-facts/.

2. Compiled from various sources, including David Lohr, *Sandy Hook Shooting Victims' Names Released*, Huffington Post (December 17, 2012).

3. Compiled from The Associated Press and *List of Virginia Tech Victims*, 6ABC.COM (April 19, 2007).

4. Kirk Johnson, *Survivors of High School Rampage Left with Injuries and Questions*, New York Times (March 25, 2005).

APPENDIX TWO. MASS SHOOTINGS IN THE UNITED STATES, 1982–2018

1. Mark Follman, Gavin Aronsen, and Deanna Pan, *US Mass Shootings, 1982–2019: Data from Mother Jones' Investigation* (February 2019), Mother Jones, https://www.motherjones.com/politics/2012/12/mass-shootings-mother-jones-full-data. *See also* Mother Jones, *A Guide To Mass Shootings in America*, (July, 2012), https://www.motherjones.com/politics/2012/07/mass-shootings-map/.

2. Lizzie Johnsen, Melody Gutierrez, and Kurtis Alexander, *Army Vet Who Killed Caregivers in Yountville Lost Guard License Amid Troubles* (Mary 12, 2018), SF Gate, https://www.sfgate.com/crime/article/yountville-shooting-Jennifer-Golick-family-victims-12747300.php.

BIBLIOGRAPHY

Over a four-year period I consulted numerous books, articles, and sources in the course of researching and writing this book. The following is by no means an exhaustive list of the works I found helpful or that influenced my thinking on the idea of the aftermath of rampage murders. It does, however, reflect the sources I either quoted directly or relied upon extensively throughout my research, as indicated in the notes accompanying the text. I also include works that readers who wish to explore this topic further may find of interest and works that are noteworthy or influential in the fields covered.

Raymond D. Austin, Navajo Courts and Navajo Common Law (2009).

Harold J. Berman, Law and Revolution: The Formation of the Western Legal Tradition, 183 (1983).

Jeanne Bishop, Change of Heart: Justice, Mercy and Making Peace with My Sister's Killer (2015).

Nils Bockler, Thorsten Seeger, Peter Sitzer, and Wilhelm Heitmeyer, eds., School Shootings: International Research, Case Studies and Concepts for Prevention (2013).

John Braithwaite, Restorative Justice and Responsive Regulation (2002).

John Braithwaite, Valerie Braithwaite, Michael Cookson, and Leah Dunn, Anomie and Violence (2010).

Dave Cullen, Columbine (2009).

Kathleen Daly, *Restorative Justice: The Real Story*, 4 Punishment & Soc'y 55 (2002).

D. E. Davis, E. L. Worthington Jr., J. N. Hook, and P. C. Hill, *Research on Religion/Spirituality and Forgiveness: A Meta-Analytic Review,* Psychology of Religion and Spirituality (2013).

R. D. Enright, *Forgiveness Is a Choice: A Step-by-Step Process for Resolving Anger and Restoring Hope*, American Psychological Association (2001).

R. Fehr, M. J. Gelfand, and M. Nag, *The Road to Forgiveness: A Meta-Analytic Synthesis of Its Situational and Dispositional Correlates*, 136 Psychological Bulletin, 894–914 (2010).

Final Report of the Sandy Hook Advisory Commission (March 6, 2015), http://www.shac.ct.gov/SHAC_Final_Report_3-6-2015.pdf.

James Alan Fox and Jack Levin, *Multiple Homicide: Patterns of Serial and Mass Murder*, 23 Crime & Just. 407 (1998).

James Alan Fox, Jack Levin, and Kenna Quinet, The Will to Kill: Making Sense of Senseless Murder (2012).

Suzanne Freedman, *Forgiveness and Reconciliation: The Importance of Understanding How They Differ*, 42 Counseling and Values (1998).

Burt Galaway and Joe Hudson, eds., Restorative Justice: International Perspectives (1996).

Carrie E. Garrow and Sarah Deer, Tribal Criminal Law and Procedure (2004).

George Bird Grinnel, The Cheyenne Indians (2 vols. 1923).

Sidney L. Harring, Crow Dog's Case: American Indian Sovereignty, Tribal Law and United States Law in the Nineteenth Century (1994).

E. Adamson Hoebel, The Law of Primitive Man (1961).

Missy Jenkins and William Coyle, I Choose to Be Happy: A School Shooting Survivor's Triumph over Tragedy (2008).

Susan Klebold, *I Will Never Know Why*, O, the Oprah Magazine (November 2009).

Susan Klebold, A Mother's Reckoning: Living in the Aftermath of Tragedy (2016).

Peter Langman, Why Kids Kill: Inside the Minds of School Shooters (2009).

Peter Langman, School Shooters: Understanding High School, College and Adult Perpetrators (2015).

Aaron Lazare, On Apology (2004).

C. G. Lee et al., *A Community Court Grows in Brooklyn: A Comprehensive Evaluation of the Red Hook Community Justice Center*, National Center for State Courts (2013), https://www.courtinnovation.org/sites/default/files/media/document/2018/RH_Report.pdf.

R. S. Littlefield, J. Reierson, K. Cowden, S. Stowman, and C. Long Feather, *A Case Study of the Red Lake, Minnesota, School Shooting: Intercultural Learning in the Renewal Process*, 2(3) Communication, Culture & Critique 361–383 (2009).

K. N. Llewellyn and E. Adamson Hoebel, The Cheyenne Way: Conflict and Case Law in
   Primitive Jurisprudence (1941).

Matthew Lysiak, Newtown: An American Tragedy (2013).

Wanda D. Mccaslin, ed., Justice as Healing: Indigenous Ways: Writings on Community
   Peacemaking and Restorative Justice from the Native Law Center (2005).

Lewis Henry Morgan, The League of the Iroquois (1851).

Native American Rights Fund (NARF), Frequently Asked Questions about Peacemaking,
   http://www.narf.org/peacemaking/learn_more/faq.html.

Navajo Nation Judicial Branch, Institutional History of *HózhÓji Naat'aah*, http://www.
   navajocourts.org/indexpeaceplanops.htm.

William B. Newell, Crime and Justice among the Iroquois Nations (1965).

Katherine S. Newman, Cybelle Fox, David J. Harding, Jal Mehta, and Wendy Roth, Rampage:
   The Social Roots of School Shootings (2004).

Marianne O. Nielson and James W. Zion, Navajo Nation Peacemaking (2005).

Mary Ellen O'Toole, *Jeffrey Weise and the Shooting at Red Lake Minnesota High School: A
   Behavioral Perspective*, in School Shootings, 178 (Nils Bockler, Thorsten Seeger, Peter Sitzer,
   and Wilhelm Heitmeyer, eds., 2013).

Alissa Parker, An Unseen Angel: A Mother's Story of Hope and Healing after Sandy Hook
   (2017).

John Pratt, *Colonization Power and Silence: A History of Indigenous Justice in New Zealand
   Society*, in Restorative Justice: International Perspectives, 138 (Burt Galaway and Joe
   Hudson, eds., 1996).

Richard E. Redding, *Why It Is Essential to Teach about Mental Health Issues in Criminal Law*, 14
   Wash. U. J. L. & Pol'y 407, 410 (2004).

Report of the Review Panel, *Mass Shootings at Virginia Tech* (August 2007).

Thomas J. Scheff, *Community Conferences: Shame and Anger in Therapeutic Jurisprudence,* 67
   Rev. Jur. U.P.R. 97-119 (1999), as reprinted in Judging in a Therapeutic Key, 231–247 (Bruce
   J. Winick and David B. Wexler, eds., 2003).

Rennard Strickland, Fire and the Spirits (1975).

Douglas Sylvester, *Myth in Restorative Justice History*, 2003 Utah L. Rev. 471 (2003).

Mark Umbreit and Marilyn Peterson Armour, Restorative Justice Dialogue: An Essential Guide
   for Research and Practice (2011).

N. G. Wade, W. T. Hoyt, J. E. M. Kidwell, and E. L. Worthington Jr., *Efficacy of Psychotherapeutic
   Interventions to Promote Forgiveness: A Meta-Analysis*. J. of Consulting & Clinical
   Psychology (2013).

Anthony F. C. Wallace, *The Career of William N. Fenton and the Development of Iroquoian*

Studies, in Extending the Rafters: Interdisciplinary Approaches to Iroquois Studies, 1 (Michael K. Foster, et al, eds., 1984)

Robert A. Williams Jr., Linking Arms Together: American Indian Treaty Visions of Law and Peace, 1600–1800 (1977).

Bruce J. Winick and David B. Wexler, eds., Judging in a Therapeutic Key (2003).

E. L. Worthington Jr., Five Steps to Forgiveness: The Art and Science of Forgiving (2001).

Howard Zehr, Changing Lenses: A New Focus for Crime and Justice (3d ed. 2005).

INDEX